First Church of Christ in Quincy

The Chapel of Eas and Church of Statesmen

First Church of Christ in Quincy

The Chapel of Eas and Church of Statesmen

ISBN/EAN: 9783744735070

Printed in Europe, USA, Canada, Australia, Japan

Cover: Foto ©ninafisch / pixelio.de

More available books at **www.hansebooks.com**

THE "CHAPPEL OF EASE"

AND

CHURCH OF STATESMEN.

Commemorative Services

AT THE

COMPLETION OF TWO HUNDRED AND FIFTY YEARS
SINCE THE GATHERING OF THE

First Church of Christ in Quincy.

WITH ILLUSTRATIONS.

PRINTED FOR THE SOCIETY.
1890.

PREFACE.

THE labor involved in getting at the facts of the HISTORY OF FIRST CHURCH, and in arranging for publication what else is in these pages, has been greatly lightened by the courteous assistance of many who are engaged in historical research, and by the encouragement of all interested in the story and fame of this ancient society.

To Mr. CHARLES FRANCIS ADAMS I am especially indebted for his co-operation in securing photographs of the portraits of his ancestors, and for the frequent use I have made of his full and very interesting sketch of Quincy in the "History of Norfolk County." This sketch I have found to be an almost exhaustless treasury of facts, well chosen and skilfully connected, and the extent of my borrowings from it has been limited only by the confined scope of this book. Mr. J. P. QUINCY readily furnished the engraving of Josiah Quincy, and from other members of his family I have obtained valuable hints. Many excellent suggestions have come to me from Mr. S. A. BATES, Braintree's noted antiquary and town clerk, and from the Hon. SAMUEL A. GREEN, Secretary of the Massachusetts Historical Society. Messrs. Houghton, Mifflin, & Co. proffered the electrotype of "Dorothy Q.;" Messrs. Ticknor & Co. permitted the use of the engraving of John Hancock, which was prepared for the "Memorial History of Boston," and the proprietors of the "Quincy Patriot" lent their electrotype of the Rev. John Hancock Meeting-House. Other illustrations I am enabled to supply from the engravings used by Dr. Lunt in the "Two Hundredth Anniversary" discourses, which were given me by Mrs. REVERE. Mr. HARRY L. RICE placed in my hands many artistic photographs of Quincy houses and their interiors, which have been of great assistance. The view of the interior of the Stone Temple was taken by him at my request. To all these and many besides who also rendered essential service my thanks are extended.

Owing to the length of the historical discourses, much in them was omitted when they were delivered. They are now published in full, with notes and an appendix.

D. M. WILSON.

QUINCY, March, 1890.

CONTENTS.

	PAGE
THE "CHAPPEL OF EASE"	1
THE CHURCH OF STATESMEN	33
COMMEMORATIVE SERVICES	65
INVOCATION BY THE REV. R. STEBBINS	69
PRAYER BY THE REV. A. P. PUTNAM, D.D.	70
ADDRESS BY THE PASTOR	73
LETTER OF GOV. OLIVER AMES	74
ADDRESS BY THE REV. S. W. BROOKE	76
REMARKS OF MR. L. H. H. JOHNSON	80
LETTER OF THE REV. J. D. WELLS	81
ADDRESS BY CHARLES FRANCIS ADAMS	82
ADDRESS BY THE REV. A. A. ELLSWORTH	87
ADDRESS BY JOSIAH QUINCY	91
POEM BY CHRISTOPHER P. CRANCH	97
ADDRESS BY THE REV. C. R. ELIOT	105
ADDRESS BY THE REV. JAMES DE NORMANDIE	108
ADDRESS BY THE REV. JOSEPH OSGOOD	110
PERSONS PRESENT AT THE 200TH AND 250TH ANNIVERSARIES	112
LETTERS OF CONGRATULATION	113
PRELIMINARY PROCEEDINGS	133

APPENDIX.

	PAGE
THE COVENANT	137
THE DEACONS	138
MEETING-HOUSES	139
GIFTS OF COMMUNION VESSELS	147
OTHER GIFTS TO THE CHURCH	150
PORTRAIT OF JOHN WHEELWRIGHT, AND OTHER PORTRAITS AND PICTURES	151
MOSES FISKE'S AUTOGRAPH	159

ILLUSTRATIONS.

	PAGE
STONE TEMPLE	*Frontispiece*
MOUNT WOLLASTON IN 1839	4
JOHN WHEELWRIGHT	12
QUINCY MANSION	17
BRACKETT HOMESTEAD	17
THE WEBB HOUSE	25
BIRTHPLACES OF JOHN AND JOHN QUINCY ADAMS	25
THE RUGGLES HOUSE	25
THE HANCOCK MEETING-HOUSE	49
JOHN ADAMS	50
ABIGAIL ADAMS	50
JOHN HANCOCK	52
JOSIAH QUINCY	54
JOHN QUINCY ADAMS	56
MRS. JOHN QUINCY ADAMS	56
CHARLES FRANCIS ADAMS	62
MRS. CHARLES FRANCIS ADAMS	62
GRAVESTONES OF PASTOR TOMPSON AND TEACHER FLYNT	64
INTERIOR OF STONE TEMPLE	65
REV. WM. SMITH	81
RICHARD CRANCH	81

ILLUSTRATIONS.

	PAGE
REV. PETER WHITNEY	81
REV. W. P. LUNT, D.D.	81
REV. J. D. WELLS	81
REV. D. M. WILSON	81
TABLET TO JOHN AND ABIGAIL ADAMS	103
TABLET TO JOHN QUINCY AND LOUISA CATHERINE ADAMS	111
INVITATION TO 250TH ANNIVERSARY	113
"DOROTHY Q."	116
ADAMS MANSION	121
DRAWING-ROOM IN ADAMS MANSION	121
YORKE COMMUNION CUP, 1699	147
CRANCH HOUSE	155
THE REV. JOHN WILSON HOUSE	155
SIGNATURE OF MOSES FISKE	159

HISTORICAL DISCOURSES.

I.

THE "CHAPPEL OF EASE."

For this is the Covenant that I will make with the House of Israel after those days, saith the Lord: I will put my Laws into their mind, and write them in their hearts. — *Hebrews* viii. 10.

FOR a church to have lived two and a half centuries of the nineteen named after Christ may seem a slight distinction, most especially when that measure of continuance is compared, to go back no further, with the age of the really ancient Christian institutions of the Old World, — such as the Cathedral of Canterbury founded by Saint Augustine, or the monastic order organized by Saint Benedict. But when it is remembered that this length of life is concurrent with the history of civilization in New England, that it was about two hundred and fifty years ago that one lofty enterprise, conceived and executed by devout and courageous men and women, established the State as well as the Church; when, too, we consider that whatever of holiest aspiration and noblest endeavor has distinguished the people of New England — their longing for things eternal, their obedience to laws human and divine, their domestic virtues, their love of liberty, their respect for learning — was kindled and nourished at the altar thus early erected to God, — then the rounding of two and a half centuries may fairly be celebrated as an event of some importance. With this regard, many of our old "First Churches" have recently observed with much solemn rejoicing their two hundred and fiftieth birthday. No church of them all, however, has, in the circumstances attending its formation, a more exciting and picturesque history than this First Church of Christ in Quincy; and no other in all the land has become more famous for eminent and entirely noble men and women. Ours is a church with a story.

Much of this story has been told on previous anniversaries by two of the most noted pastors of the church, — the Rev. John Hancock, and the Rev. William P. Lunt, D. D. Their careful and eloquent discourses have served greatly to deepen affection for this ancient society, and to increase the devotion of its members to the pure principles of our religion. All that is left me to do now is to cherish the hope that I may improve in some slight measure the present occasion as they worthily improved the past occasions.

Exciting were the circumstances, I have said, which attended the formation of this church. It was here, in this place, that the stern temper and solidifying dogmatism of the Puritan came in conflict, on two notable occasions, with more free and fluent conceptions of life and belief. Had these attained permanence and power the course of New England history would have been changed materially. Certainly one of the movements which they opposed would have, in the tolerant and expanding spirit of it, so allayed the fierce dogmatic zeal of the Puritans, that the ruthless persecution of Quakers, Baptists, and so-called witches might never have stained the otherwise whitest character of the founders of our institutions.

MORTON AND MERRYMOUNT.

The first thing with which the ideas of the Puritans clashed was a conception of life. As they would put it, it was a matter, not of doctrine, but of practice. Morton's enterprise at Merrymount was in the serious motive of it a trading adventure, and in the lighter aspects of it a transplanted bit of the boisterous life of the unregenerate Englishman of that time, who became King's man and Cavalier in contemptuous enmity to all those he called "fanatics." Judged by any standard some of the practices of Morton and his fellows are reprehensible, but surely they are made to assume a darker shade contrasted with the stern ambition and irreproachable life of the other settlers in the Bay. These jovial spirits, to whom it was imputed a sin to dance around a May-pole, were no worse than the average non-Puritan, good-easy Englishman who did the same thing on the village green across the sea. Taken back to England charged by the Puritans with grievous faults, Morton passes for a law-abiding person. Returning once more to these shores, black again he appears against the white ground of the theocracy. However we may think of this, is it not, at least, to be admitted that the revels of the adventurers at Merrymount were tempered with poetry and the classics? And does not Morton claim for himself that one of his chief functions was to "endeavor to advance the dignity of the Church of England and the laudable use of the Book of Common Prayer"? Had these mis-

MERRYMOUNT.

sionaries of "Merrie England" conducted themselves less dissolutely, is it not probable they still would have been an abomination in the sight of the Puritans? Was it not the kind of their offence more than the degree of their offending which incensed Bradford, Endicott, and the rest? Sternly the Puritans had renounced everything for the dogma that earthly existence, being under the curse, is a term of perilous probation, from which they were to be rescued by the one narrow outlet of justification. What cared they for the pastimes, or even the intellectual delights, of a world thus darkened by sin and endangering their eternal welfare! Its pleasures, its beauty, its art, its graces were worse than vanities. They might be temptations of the Evil One. How much thought loses in breadth and sympathy, and life in adornment and comfort, by thus being given over to dogma, I will not pause to show. However admirable their resolute strength of character and the singleness of their devotion, it is plain they left one side of their being entirely uncultivated. The more rigid of them could not look patiently upon even the innocent enjoyment of this life and the good things of it. We do not condemn them for this. They were so terribly in earnest to settle exactly right their relations to God, and to save themselves wholly from the power of Satan, that everything outside the sphere of these efforts seemed beyond expression inane. While in England they regarded with pity or ineffable scorn the men who indulged in pleasure, — it is to be admitted it was often sinful pleasure, — and when they found the same sort here in this New World they felt under no restraint to tolerate such "vile persons and loose-livers." And very likely it were wisest to conclude that in solemn times of sternest endeavor mocking "fribbles," and "debauchees" however amusing, are forthwith to be banished.[1] Here is the motive which prompted hostility to Morton; and when he made himself really culpable by selling fire-arms to the savages, the occasion was quickly seized. From Pascataway to Plymouth the settlers united to cast out this swaggering sportsman, this exponent of pleasant living and "the laudable use of the Book of Common Prayer." John Fiske

[1] C. F. Adams's Introduction to New English Canaan.

calls him a "picturesque but ill-understood personage." An ill-used personage he was now to be also. Miles Standish, with his "invincible army," invaded our soil, captured Morton, and roughly dragged him to Plymouth. Thence he was shipped a prisoner to England. He returned free the next year, only to be seized by the Boston magistrates, imprisoned, put in the bilboes, and to England sent once more. As he passed out of the bay his house was fired in his sight, in rough intimation that the "fanatic separatists" had done with him for good and all; that "the habitation of the wicked should no more appear in Israel;" and that henceforth this land was to be given up to sobriety of carriage and the preaching of the accepted dogma.

After the dispersion of Morton and his "consorts," the country round about the Mount was practically unoccupied by the whites. It was known chiefly now as the planting ground of the tribe of Indians called the Massachusetts, and through its meadows and around the head of its salt-water inlets was worn the trail which ran between Plymouth and Boston. If a few of Morton's party still lingered upon the lands he claimed, they have left no trace to assure us of the fact. The raids of Miles Standish and the Boston magistrates were only too effectual in cutting off ten years from the age of this settlement, and making us the fifteenth or so, when we might have been the first or second, in the Bay. But as recompense the soil was to be planted with better seed. God was "sifting a whole nation that he might send choice grain over into this wilderness."

THE BRAINTREE COMPANY.

In the summer of 1632 the company — or congregation, rather — of the renowned minister, the Rev. Thomas Hooker, from Braintree in Essex County, England, began to "sit down" at the Mount and provide for the coming of their pastor and still others of the brethren. While they were actively engaged erecting houses to shelter them during the approaching winter, word came in August from the General Court that they were to remove to Newtown, now Cambridge. They did not depart at once, we surmise, for it is likely they would keep to the rude shelter already begun, and improve it throughout the short season left them. There is no evidence the allotments were made at Newtown and the names of those taking them recorded before the next spring. And not all, who went thither, removed at last to Hartford when Hooker led the Braintree company there. Two, we certainly know, drifted to Hingham.[1] Some we must presume remained here. The fact that eight years later the town when incorporated was called Braintree, is evidence that settlers from Hooker's company continued here and acquired influence. We may reasonably account this the beginning of the permanent settlement at the Mount.

THE MOUNT ANNEXED TO BOSTON.

Hooker was a noted divine, and his people entirely worthy persons. But a more important company still

[1] Page's History of Cambridge.

was about this time looked for from England. One wonders if the Braintree company was ordered away to make room for it. John Cotton, the famous rector of St. Botolph's, in Boston, England, was coming over, and with him many others, some being wealthy and influential. Where should they be bestowed? The arrival of Cotton in September, 1633, and about two hundred more made this question urgent. At once the Governor and Council, together with the ministers and elders of all the churches, met to consider the matter. The new arrivals desired they "might sit down where they might keep store of cattle." Boston, with scarce seven hundred acres, and much of that marsh and rough thicket, had no sufficient accommodation. But in Boston the great Cotton and his company must be retained. So "it was agreed by full consent that the fittest place for him was Boston, and in that respect [of scarcity of land] those of Boston might take farms in any part of the Bay not belonging to other towns."[1] Cotton was then added to the Boston church as Teacher, and the General Court in the spring of 1634 ordered that "Boston shall have convenient enlargement at Mount Wollaston." Four "indifferent men" were appointed to draw up a plan of the lands there and apportion them. Men not "indifferent" there were, who had already fixed their desires upon certain choice portions of the newly acquired territory.[2] These were to be provided for. But first their respect

---

[1] Winthrop, i. 133.
[2] December. First. 1634. — It is granted that Mr. Newbery shall have the hedgey ground that lies in the bottom betwixt his house and the water next Mr. Cottington's farme in p'te of the medow that he is to have. — *Dorchester Record.*

for the ministry found expression in a large grant of land to their pastor, John Wilson, then absent on a voyage to England to bring over his wife. Already he had received land by Mystic side, but now on the 10th of December, 1634, there were bestowed upon him as many acres "at his election" in this favored place as his former grant amounted to, and in exchange for it. He returned in October of 1635, and seeking to possess himself of his allotment found it encumbered with the claims of earlier settlers from Dorchester and the original rights of the Indians. Evidently it was not given him to take land anywhere "at his election," but only where it was set apart for him on the plan. A matter of foreordination seems to have predominated his power of "election," — an association of these doctrines not entirely acceptable to the Boston theologian. However, to compensate him for money spent in purchasing the rights of claimants he was permitted to keep his land by Mystic, and additional acres were granted him at the Mount. Ten days after this was done there was "bound out there what may be sufficient for Mr. William Coddington and Edmund Quinsey to have for their particular farms there." For situation their allotment excelled, and we hear not an echo of conflicting claims. These were the men not "indifferent," who were not, for fairness' sake, to be appointed on the committee to draw up a plan, yet who, long before this, had selected their lands and purchased all rights of Indians and others. Coddington was the treasurer of the colony, a man of substance and solid influence, noted too as builder of the first brick house in Boston. Quincy was also a man of means and commanding character, chosen to office soon after his arrival here. The grant these two men received amounted to above a thousand acres in one broad strip bordering on the sea, and extending from Sachem's Brook to a point beyond the hill which Morton made famous.

These prior claims settled, Boston was ready to give members of Cotton's company and others of its own congregation sufficient allotments. Atherton Hough, sometime mayor of Boston, England, and a man of consequence among Cotton's followers, had laid out for him a large estate of six hundred acres on the Neck, to this day named after him. Another devoted adherent of Cotton was William Hutchinson. His wife, who was more devoted still, and who welcomed the wilderness that had Cotton to preach in it, was the famous Anne Hutchinson, so prominent later in the first great doctrinal controversy of the colony. This William Hutchinson received a "great lott" adjoining Wilson's grant on the west, in what is now North Quincy and East Milton. At the same time that these large grants were made, three divisions of allotments were marked out for the "common people."[1] These allotments were apportioned at the rate of seven acres for every person in the family, and were arranged along Town River and mostly to the south of it. They were called the "Brethren's Lots," for all receiving them were members of the Boston congregation. It is a notable fact that only such as were members of the congregation, or likely to be, were granted lands. A church was settling here,— a congregation of earnest persons who could no longer

[1] Boston Records, pp. 21, 46, 47.

endure in silence the candles, the posturing, and the doctrines imposed by the bishops, and who, not caring to abide the perils of open speech (the imprisonment, the whipping, the maiming, which Laud imposed), had fled for peace to this wide and free wilderness. With all their home-making, still uppermost in their thoughts were spiritual things. They were so disposing themselves as best "to worship God and enjoy him forever." As yet their meeting-house was in Boston, and thither on the Lord's Day they conscientiously repaired. But so rapid was the growth of the new settlement that two years had not elapsed since the first allotment was made, when the inhabitants were petitioning to be set off as an independent town and church. In December of 1636 eight persons, with the Governor at their head, were chosen to consider "of Mount Wollastone business, and for the ripening thereof how there may be a town and church there with the consent of this town's inhabitants."[1] "Many meetings were about it. The great let was, in regard it was given to Boston for upholding the town and church there, which end would be frustrated by the removal of so many chief men as would go thither. For help of this it was propounded that such as dwelt there should pay six-pence the acre, yearly, for such lands as lay within a mile of the water, and three-pence for that which lay farther off."[2]

All conspired to the speedy establishment here of one of the most prosperous and progressive towns in the colony. The "chief men," intelligent, ambitious, and wealthy, were here; the people, sober and industrious,

[1] Boston Records, p. 14.   [2] Winthrop, i. 233.

were here in sufficient and increasing numbers. All the preliminaries were arranged; actually all but the final step taken. A church too was virtually gathered, and only waited for that joining in solemn covenant which should launch it into an independent and influential career. Indeed, the very character of that church seemed to be determined. For some time now, events in the colony had been bringing to the surface the progressive and conservative instincts of the people and arraying them in opposing parties. And as a number of the more liberal sort had already established themselves at the Mount, others were looking in that direction as to a retreat for the peaceful development of their opinions. The right minister only seemed wanting, but he also was at hand in Boston, — a man by temperament and scholarship fitted to lead an intelligent, truth-seeking congregation. The next month he received an invitation to labor at the Mount.

JOHN WHEELWRIGHT.

The Rev. John Wheelwright arrived in Boston with his family the 26th of May, 1636, about seven months before the committee was chosen to arrange for an independent church at the Mount. He was at this time forty-four years of age, in the full strength of manhood, energetic, independent, aggressive. Oliver Cromwell was his college classmate and friend; they were alike in the fearlessness and stubbornness of their character. Persistently Wheelwright preached against the ceremonial innovations of Laud, and when silenced for it resolutely turned his

John Wheelwright

HELIOTYPE PRINTING CO., BOSTON.

face to the New World. He found affairs not entirely
peaceful here. Mrs. Hutchinson, "his sister," as Winthrop called her (Mr. Hutchinson was his wife's brother),
was beginning to attract attention by her original ideas,
and by daring to criticise some of the ministers. Now
two years in the colony, she by her tender, neighborly
offices had endeared herself as "a dear saint and servant
of God," as her husband described her; and by her bright
intelligence had become a necessity to women spiritually
perplexed. Woman then, as regards religion at least,
was the suppressed sex, quite silently subservient to the
solemn ecclesiastical routine, her spontaneity and swift
instincts obstructed by ponderous masculine formality.
With all a woman's disdain of mechanism, Mrs. Hutchinson expressed in the most luminous way just what was
in the minds of her sisters, and then led them on to
higher interpretations of the letter and finer perceptions
of the spirit. She was interesting; they liked to hear
her talk, and gained more profit from her than from the
most "painful preaching." In time, as Winthrop declares,
" she had more resort to her for counsel about matters of
conscience than any minister (I might say all the elders)
in the country." And from a few who dropped in to talk
with her about the sermons preached of a Sunday or lecture day, she eventually gathered around her, twice in
the week regularly, as many as from sixty to a hundred
women. This went on at first with the entire commendation of the ministers. It was like a modern revival.
But trouble began when Mrs. Hutchinson discovered that
Pastor Wilson's preaching was not so spiritual as that
of her favorite divine, Teacher Cotton. She criticised

other ministers too; said they preached a "covenant of works," and hinted that an austere countenance was no sure sign of piety.

The ministers of the colony were a peculiar class, exalted by their sacrifices for the faith of the Reformers, and reverenced as the prophets, the very mouths of God. "What ye do unto them, the Lord Jesus takes as done unto himself," was gravely asserted. "And now suddenly," as Mr. C. F. Adams the younger writes, "a woman came, and calmly and persistently intimated that as a class God's prophets in New England were not what they seemed." This was more than could be borne by even "very humble and unworthy instruments of God." To teach strange doctrine was bad enough, but to doubt the accredited servants of the Most High was worse. Fairly, however, they were open to this criticism. The weak and disagreeable side of Puritanism was its insistence upon uniformity in doctrine and the upholding of the ordinances. The same phrases were expected from every one, the same outward demeanor, the same pious routine. One might make a business of all this, go through it mechanically, appear to be very devout, and still remain unspiritual within.

From this the teaching of Mrs. Hutchinson was a revolt. She laid the emphasis upon spirituality. No matter about the outward demeanor and the painful effort to fulfil the law. Have the heart right; let the spiritual principle be active within you, — then whatever is worthy and of good report will follow. She really rose to a sublime religious philosophy when she declared that the individual might have union with the Holy Spirit, and that then he is more than a creature: he is immortal, has present revelations of God, and is filled with ravishing joy. What have we better than that to-day? To be sure, when one attempts to define such union he is liable to ambiguity of expression; and when he tries to extort too much from private revelations he is likely to fall into extravagances. In these particulars the Hutchinson party exposed themselves to misunderstandings. Nevertheless here was a genuine advance of the Spirit, a genial enlightenment in the natural evolution of the Puritan ideal.

Wheelwright allied himself at once and enthusiastically with the "Covenant of Grace" party. Not that Mrs. Hutchinson now converted him. These heart-searching principles were held in common by them both and by others while in England. They might almost be called the Lincolnshire varient of non-conformity. All the Hutchinsons held it to be the truth. Cotton and Hough and others from the fens district were sympathetic, and doubtless Wheelwright during the three years he lived near Lincoln under the ban of the bishops labored as he did in this land "to bring Christ into the hearts of the people." By not one of the liberals is this doctrine introduced as a thing strange and revolutionary. It is regarded by them simply as the ideal puritanism, the faith of the Reformers at its best, the *truth*, the hope of the free enjoyment of which had brought them all to this country. Why it should give offence to any was no doubt a surprise to Wheelwright. On the side of this vital and sincere effort to realize God in the heart he found arrayed the entire Boston church, with the exception of Wilson the pastor, Governor Winthrop, and one or two others. "Many out of the church were her converts; yea," says Winthrop, bitterly, "many profane persons became of her opinion." It was a popular movement sweeping into its current the chief town in the Bay, and some in other towns. Glad to find Wheelwright with them, this party was minded to place him with Wilson and Cotton as a third minister over Boston church. On a Sunday in the October after his arrival this project was set in motion, and on the 30th was taken up for definite action. Opposition was made; even Cotton, who was claimed by the liberals, saying he "could not consent, . . . calling in one whose spirit they knew not, and one who seemed to dissent in judgment; . . . and though he thought reverently of his godliness and abilities, so as he could be content to live under such a ministry, yet seeing he was apt to raise doubtful disputations he could not consent to choose him to that place. . . . Whereupon the church gave way that he might be called to a new church to be gathered at Mount Wollaston."

WHEELWRIGHT CALLED TO THE MOUNT.

The promptness with which Wheelwright was diverted from Boston church to the church growing up at the Mount suggests it was a purpose held in hand as a second resort by the liberals. I am tempted to say that the intention was becoming manifest to build in this place a church in which the new spirit and expanding views might be peaceably unfolded. At all events the enterprise

THE OLDER QUINCY MANSION.

THE BRACKETT HOMESTEAD

of a new church and town ripened rapidly. It was about a month after Wheelwright began to labor here, in December of 1636, that the eight persons with the Governor at their head were chosen " to consider of Mount Wollaston business, — how there may be a church and town there." At this time Wheelwright lodged, perhaps, as the occasion required, in Coddington's house, by " Mount Wollastone River;" and it may be the preaching at first was done in the same place.[1] But now the minister was to have an estate and house of his own. In the February following, Coddington and Wright were ordered to lay out for him where most convenient, " without prejudice to setting up of a town there," two hundred and fifty acres. At the same time others who confided in him and followed him, applied for and received allotments.[2] The Wheelwright grant started with forty acres in the three-hill marsh, with five acres for house-lot (where perhaps the old Brackett homestead now is), and two hundred and five acres at the end of it extending into the country. Here, by the banks of " Town Brook "

[1] That Coddington then had a house at the Mount is made clear by what Lechford records in his Note Book. Wm. Tyng, who subsequently purchased the Coddington estate, wants to lease it to a Mr. Reade. One of the conditions is that Reade shall allow Tyng entertainment when he visits the farm, "and at these times he shall have the use of the chamber which Mr. Coddington used to lye in for his lodging." There was also a large barn. The buildings were situated about where the old Quincy mansion is on Black's Creek. The stream was first called Mount Wollaston River, then Coddington's Brook, next Quincy's Brook, and since, after every occupant of the historic house there. The latest appellation is Butler's Brook. This home-lot between brook and pond and near tide-landing, and with extensive meadows on every hand, was the prize place in the plantation.

[2] Among these Nicholas Needham, William Wardwell, a servant of Edmund Quincy, and William Cole are found with Wheelwright when he went to Exeter.

running through "the heart" of the settlement, was his farm; and here he began at once to make a home for wife and children, and to root himself in our soil. Regularly he ministered to the congregation gathering about him, winning the confidence of his people, and working together with them to establish a choice community. In this very beginning of our church it was, for numbers, quite strong. Besides those of the Mount it included, probably, some of Dorchester's people living this side the Neponset, and some from Weymouth, where they too "had drunk in some of Mrs. Hutchinson's opinions." But however large, it was not yet an independent church; it was only what Lawyer Lechford called a "CHAPPEL OF EASE, . . . where a neighboring minister or brother preacheth and exerciseth prayer every Lord's day," the people still members of Boston church, and as sign of that receiving the sacrament there.

SWORDS IN A SERMON.

On a fast, kept Jan. 19, 1636, most, it may be, went to Boston to "receive." At all events their minister was there, for in the afternoon, after Mr. Cotton had preached a "directive" sermon on reconciliation, "Mr. Wheelwright was desired by the church to exercise as a private brother by way of prophecy." Whereupon he pushed his way slowly to the pulpit through the crowded congregation which filled Boston's primitive meeting-house, took a sermon from his pocket and spread it before him. Eager and alert were the faces he looked upon. Already that day the people

had listened to two long discourses,[1] and to as many
prayers, "unmerciful" in their length, as the unsympathetic Lechford describes them. Still, they were hungry
to hear more with regard to the controversy which
agitated the town, and were in strained expectancy of
word or phrase which, according to their bias, would
be either luminous with truth or dark with heresy.
Wheelwright felt the stimulus of the occasion. His
sermon, written at a hint that it would be called for,
he preached with fervency. Although he girded vigorously against "legalists," — all "those under a covenant
of works," — he was wholly unconscious that he was
uttering anything incendiary. And yet no other sermon ever preached on this continent has had such a
remarkable effect. Immediately it arrayed "legalists"
in open and concerted hostility against "antinomians,"
and brought the colony to the very verge of ruin.
Read that sermon carefully and you will see it is a
quite sensible production, written closely to the occasion, and having for chief exhortation the "keeping
Christ in a spiritual way." You may discern a thread
of fire running through its uncouth phraseology; but
there is really not enough flame in it to account for
the great conflagration which ensued. To be sure he
says, "We must all prepare for a spiritual combat;"
to "keep the Lord Jesus Christ," the children of God
"ought to show themselves valiant; they should have
their swords ready; they must fight, and fight with
spiritual weapons." Of course the "swords" are figurative, and the warfare which was urged a wordy one.

[1] Mercurius Americanus, p. 216, in C. H. Bell's "Life of J. Wheelwright."

But the "legalists," affronted anew by so fearless an arraignment of such as opposed "free grace" on an occasion so notable, and alarmed at the formidable proportions to which the new movement was attaining, were disposed to take them in a literal sense. Something must be done to suppress the heresy. As Mr. C. F. Adams the younger says, "they greatly needed a scapegoat; and a scapegoat they found ready to their hands in the pastor at the Mount."

Wheelwright, conscious only that on a distinguished occasion he had creditably delivered himself in dutiful obedience to "an over-ruling conscience," returned quietly to his labors here. Those of the other party were active, however; they took up and tossed about the martial phrases of his sermon, wrought themselves by this exercise into a condition to proceed to extremities, and spread among themselves "a silent decree that Wheelwright was to be disciplined." Concerted action brought all the ministers of the Bay together at the next meeting of the General Court, March 9, 1637. It was nearly all the colony against the Boston congregation and the congregation at the Mount. Some of the laity in Roxbury, Dorchester, Salem, and other towns took part with the liberals, but to a man the ministers outside of Boston and the Mount were bitterly antagonistic. Reason for this is found in the fact that their authority as a class seemed questioned, and their plan of a theocracy seemed imperilled. Also, it must be admitted, that many of them were absolutely bigoted in their conservatism. "I will petition to be chosen the universal idiot of the world," said

Ward of Ipswich, "if all the wits under the heavens can lay their heads together and find an assertion worse than this, — that men ought to have liberty of their conscience, and that it is persecution to debar them of it." Welde of Roxbury and Shepard of Cambridge had no words to express their condemnation of Mrs. Hutchinson when she denied the resurrection of the body; and when she avowed the belief, now held by many Christians of all sects, that "the coming of Christ is his coming to us in union," Wilson cried out, "I hold this opinion to be dangerous and damnable, and to be no less than Sadduceeism and atheism, and therefor to be detested." At the hands of such, those of liberal opinion would fare hard.

THE INQUISITION IN NEW ENGLAND.

Before a court thus constituted in the majority of it Wheelwright was summoned. The doors were closed, and he was called upon to "satisfy the court about some passages of his sermon which seemed to be offensive." He declined to give answer to a body so inquisitorial, and a petition was presented, signed by more than forty members of the Boston church, praying that the doors be opened. The petition was at first ignored; but finally the doors were thrown open, and a great and excited assembly filled the meeting-house. Again the sermon was produced, and it was charged that Wheelwright had "inveighed against all that walked in a covenant of works, had called them anti-Christs, and had stirred up the people against them."

He justified his sermon, and stoutly declared that if any did walk in a covenant of works them he did mean. What the court sought to prove was that Wheelwright's words were not to be taken in a general sense, but were particularly directed against his brother ministers. And now these ministers were asked "if they in their ministry did walk in such a way?" They desired a season to consider the matter; but as they were the chief prosecutors, it was no surprise when they uprose in the full company of them, Cotton only excepted, and with one voice acknowledged they did. "So after much debate the court adjudged him guilty of sedition and also of contempt." Coddington was a member of that court, and, as Mr. C. H. Bell points out, has left his testimony that he and Governor Vane and most of the laymen were opposed to the condemnation of Wheelwright; "but the priests got two of the magistrates on their side, and so got the major part of them." Then a remonstrance, entirely respectful in its character, was signed by about sixty of the Boston laymen. It testified to Wheelwright's peaceful and spiritual intentions. The most the court could be moved to do was to defer sentence till its next session, and barely restrained itself from imitating the bishops in their tyranny and silencing their victim. He, still astonished that his sermon should have been so ill-construed, returned to his labors at the Mount, where, nothing subdued, "he openly protested against the errors with which he was charged."[1]

The General Court at its next session, May 17, 1637,

[1] Mercurius Americanus, p. 191, in C. H. Bell's "Life of J. Wheelwright."

was ordered to meet at New Town, now Cambridge.
Boston too entirely sided with the liberals to suit the
majority. It was a court of elections; but before proceeding with that business Governor Vane and others
attempted to present a petition in behalf of Wheelwright and in defence of liberty of speech. Their
hope was in the people, and in their sense of fair play
and regard for the freedom of Englishmen. But the
"priests" were out in force; Pastor Wilson climbed
a tree and harangued the multitude. After a bitter
struggle the liberal party was defeated, and Vane and
Coddington and "all of that faction," wrote Winthrop
in triumph, "were left quite out." As there was soon
to be a fast in which it would be convenient to confer about differences, "the court gave Wheelwright
respite to the next session in August to bethink himself, that, retracting and reforming his error, the court
might show him favor, which otherwise he must not
expect. His answer was, that if he had committed
sedition then he ought to be put to death; and if we
did mean to proceed against him, he meant to appeal
to the King's Court, for he would retract nothing."[1]
On May 24, the day of the fast, Vane and Coddington, to emphasize their dissent from the methods of
their opponents, ignored the Boston assembly and its
conference and kept the day at the Mount with Mr.
Wheelwright. A pleasant memory is it to cherish, that
the pure and high-minded Sir Harry Vane, — a hero
unsurpassed in that heroic time, the fearless and farseeing statesman of the Puritan revolution, — found in

[1] Winthrop, i. 265.

the little gathering of worshippers at the Mount the one church in New England entirely congenial to his broad sympathies and tolerant spirit! No doubt the "Chappel of Ease" was filled that day with the friends of light and liberty. Stout Deacon Bass of Roxbury church was there, perhaps, with others of such as were afterward excommunicated for their opinions. Perhaps some were there from Weymouth and Dorchester. At all events it was a notable day in our ecclesiastical history, and Wheelwright had hearers not a few.

That day of humiliation had no peaceful issue. Instead, the strife deepened and extended. The conservatives sat in the seats of the magistrates; and when in July there arrived from England a ship in which were friends of the liberals, they were not permitted to land. It was a monstrous act of injustice. Not knowing to what a pass affairs had come in the colony, these people had forsaken their pleasant homes and come to these shores for peace and freedom. To their surprise they found, instead, an oppression as harsh as that exercised by the prelates, and a reception more inhospitable than that of the rude sea to which they were again driven. Cotton was so grieved that he was minded to leave the plantation. Vane in an outburst of indignation protested against the outrage, and pleaded for tolerance. His words fell upon ears deaf to everything but what "is usual among us," upon hearts hardened by dogma. Altogether disappointed he returned to England, where high political ideals beckoned him on to his tragic end.

John Quincy Adams.   John Adams
BIRTHPLACES OF PRESIDENTS

WEBB HOUSE.

Rear View   Front
ADAMS HOUSE.
Now owned by Mr. J. H. Adams and Miss E. C. Adams

Relieved of his presence, the ecclesiastical machine in all its ponderousness and solemnity was set in motion to put an end to all heresy. A synod of all the churches, the first of its kind in this new world, met at New Town (Cambridge) the 30th of August, 1637. For three weeks it sat in session, raking together all the "erroneous opinions" which partisanship had charged against the liberals. They were found to be eighty in number, to say nothing of "nine unwholesome expressions." When the slander and the gossip and the misunderstandings were abstracted from these, they were reduced to just three points of difference between Wheelwright and the rest of the ministers. Nevertheless, the eighty and nine opinions and expressions were condemned; Wheelwright was condemned, and Mrs. Hutchinson's meetings were "agreed to be disorderly and without rule." The Boston members, including those from Mount Wollaston, calling for witnesses to the eighty errors and the names of such as made charges, and being persistently refused, retired early from the synod. The remainder then "carried on matters so peaceably, and concluded them so comfortably in love," to use Winthrop's words, that they were of opinion that all was now settled, — that by the resolution of a synod thinking had been abolished, and the free spirit of man effectually harnessed to dogma. "But," laments Winthrop, "it fell out otherwise. For though Mr. Wheelwright and those of his party had been clearly confuted and confounded, yet they persisted in their opinions." To the congregation at the Mount its minister "continued his preaching after his former manner." Here he always found sympathy, and to a right understanding of his doctrines could confidently appeal at a later day.

THE FIRST MEETING-HOUSE BUILT.

It was at this time, the spring and summer of 1637, that the first meeting-house for worshippers in this place was built. There is no evidence for this, but probability favors it. The meeting-house is a recognized land-mark when the town records begin in 1640. The energetic Wheelwright would surely do his uttermost to have a place in which to shelter his congregation; and we may presume that his prominent parishioners who were looking to this place as their home, — Coddington, Mrs. Judith Quincy,[1] the Hutchinsons, Sargent Savage, and others, — would ably second his efforts. The house was situated just to the south of the bridge which then crossed Town River on the highway to Weymouth and Plymouth. It was solidly built of stone, — whether for defence against the Indians or as evidence of the deliberate purpose and settled feelings of those who were to occupy it, we cannot tell. At all events it was, so far as we know, the first stone meeting-house built in New England. For a hundred years it served the religious and civic occasions of the town, and was then superseded by the house built in 1732, under the ministry of the Rev. John Hancock.

[1] Edmund Quincy died in 1635, leaving a widow and two children "in the wilderness."

After the synod, religious matters could not be left in their unsettled state, — Mrs. Hutchinson still expounding at Boston, and Wheelwright preaching other offensive sermons at the Mount. For two months more they were tolerated; and then when the court met in November it was decisively resolved to uproot all heresy, swiftly and thoroughly.

LIBERALS DISARMED AND BANISHED.

No Star Chamber ever flung bolt more ruthless than that which was now hurled by "saints against saints." The sentence hanging over the head of Wheelwright was let fall; he was disfranchised and banished. Mrs. Hutchinson was banished. Then the sixty leading men of Boston who had mildly remonstrated that Wheelwright was peaceful and guiltless of sedition, were treated as criminals, all of them disarmed, and the more prominent banished also. The excuse for this act of tyranny was that the magistrates feared an uprising. They had indeed, through their injustice, cause to fear it; yet no liberal of them all ever made the least show of violence, and with one exception none of them ever exhibited any loose behavior. In the turbulent history of religion it was once more the resort to force of a stronger party, to rid itself of those differing from it in opinion. The churches followed up the banishments by excommunicating all their members who had manifested independence or liberality. It was wintertime, and the snow lay deep; but scourged by the oppressor, some of the worthiest of those who sought here a haven of rest must face once more the wilderness. Wheelwright, the fearless preacher of "Christ in the life;" Coddington, the independent and able counsellor; John Coggeshall, stout of heart and outspoken; the Hutchinsons, all of them high-minded and truth-loving, — these and others must leave the homes they had founded in hope and affection, their property sacrificed, or actually confiscated. "Because it was winter," Mrs. Hutchinson was not immediately driven forth, but was put in the keeping of her enemies, who tortured her with questions, confutations, and censures. She was alone, and entirely at their mercy. Her husband and her stanchest friends were in Rhode Island, negotiating for the purchase from the Indians of Acquidneck. Even her pastor, John Cotton, for whose ministrations she had crossed the ocean, deserted her, and "admonished her with much zeal and detestation of her errors." After trying her at two church-meetings, during which Welde and Shepard and Wilson and other ministers displayed their skill in ensnaring, browbeating, and confusing her whom in contempt they called "but a woman," she was solemnly excommunicated, — in set words delivered up to Satan, and "in the name of Christ commanded as a leper to withdraw herself out of the congregation." So the weary woman before the winter had quite gone, in the spring of 1638, "went by water to her farm at the Mount," and then "by land to Providence, and so to the island in the Narragansett Bay which her husband and the rest of that sect had purchased of the Indians." Further we might follow her, and tell of her wanderings and of her tragic death at the hands of the savages; but it pertains not to our history, and is all sad enough.

Wheelwright had been given fourteen days in which he was to settle his affairs and leave the colony. Upon his own request he was dismissed to his family at the Mount, his parishioner, Atherton Hough, becoming bondsman for him. Here in his own home, and surrounded by sympathizing friends, he prepared for his departure. Others also were going, and there was much sad work and sorrowful parting to do. On the last Sunday before he went he gathered his little congregation once more about him, and preached his farewell sermon. It is on record that he retracted nothing, and even more sturdily than ever defended himself against unjust charges, and expounded his ideal puritanism. It was the last sermon he ever preached at the Mount; it was the last to be preached in the little church there for some time.

Leaving his wife and children, Wheelwright set out with some voluntary exiles of his flock for Pascataway, the coast region of what is now New Hampshire. It was bitter cold, and the snow lay unusually deep, so that as he afterward declared, it was marvellous he got thither at all. There he and his companions from the Mount, together with some who came in that ship whose passengers were refused a landing, bought a large tract of country of the Indians, laid the foundations of the important settlement of Exeter, New Hampshire, and established the first church of it. Mrs. Hutchinson had intended to join him there, and she was to sail from the Mount with his wife and children; but as we have seen, she and her husband eventually threw in their lot with the Rhode

Island exiles. And now in this same spring of 1638 Wheelwright's wife with her children and his mother, accompanied by other families of the pioneers, left to join their husbands in the new plantation in the north.

THE LIBERAL PARTY CHARACTERIZED.

So with a heavy hand the "Chappel of Ease" at the Mount was abolished. For the second time the sterner spirit of the Puritan lifted itself in anger against this place, and for the second time its inhabitants were swept away. The exodus from the Mount was large and important, those cast out being since reckoned among the honorable founders of two such considerable places as Newport, Rhode Island, and Exeter, New Hampshire. We have ever since suffered from the loss; and the injury done the entire colony by the rough discomfiture and banishment of these sincere disciples of light and liberty cannot be measured. They were taking the next step in the logical development of the faith of the Reformers. The ministers were content to stay with what was "usually held among them;" the "authority of the Scriptures" was wholly in the interpretations they had already made. With this persuasion Puritanism was a closed thing, incapable of progress and prone to persecution. But in the Wheelwright party was the manifestation of growth. They were not only open to new thoughts, but were advocates of the freedom of thought itself. The right of free speech, the principle of toleration, the privilege of every man to do his own thinking and his own interpreting,— these are the things which break in light from the darkness of that controversy. Do not think that those sensible, those intelligent laymen of Boston church and other churches in the Bay were carried away with some fanciful doctrine no one now cares about. No, it was not that. Though the new ideas appealed to their mind and conscience, what most profoundly stirred them was the assault upon the dearly cherished freedom of Englishmen. They demanded fair play, they resisted tyranny. Much as they revered their ministers they could not endure their dictum that it was "corrupt judgment and practice" to question what minister or magistrate said or did. Mrs. Hutchinson precisely expressed their sentiments, when she said in her defence that "it was never in her heart to slight any man, but only that man should be kept in his own place and not set in the room of God."

THEY "STILL LIVE!"

The class which presumed to lift itself "in the room of God" had its way; the advocates of individual freedom were suppressed. We cherish the conviction, however, that not in vain they strove against tyranny. We love to think that in this church, especially, their influence is still potent. To make this plain, what can I do better than to quote the words of Charles F. Adams the younger, from whom I have already obtained so much?

"Since its foundation this parish," he writes, "has shown always a noticeable leaning toward a liberal theology. It was never Orthodox. In this respect it was in sharp contrast with its sister church of the Middle Precinct, and the ministers of the two, never changing sides, more than once engaged in sharp doctrinal controversy. And so each successive pastor influenced the people, and the tendency of the people operated back in the selection of pastors, until the old order of things passed wholly away. It is therefore no improbable surmise, that a little leaven in this case also leavened the whole lump; the seed sown by Wheelwright in 1637 bore its fruit in the great New England protest of two centuries later, when, under the lead of Channing, the descendants in the seventh generation of those who had listened to the first pastor at the Mount broke away finally and forever from the religious tenets of the Puritans." [1]

Assent we readily to all that; and may we not also surmise that civil as well as ecclesiastical history is indebted, in the development of its higher and ideal principles, to this early infusion of the spirit of independence and respect for soul liberty? Into what other ancient church of all the land has there been born so great a number of notable men with an even instinctive hatred of oppression and love of freedom? We need not recite their names or their deeds, — they shine with seven-fold light in the splendor of our greatest national achievements. We cannot stop to praise them; but they summon us to present duty, and to exercise the privilege of honoring our high traditions by loyalty to truth and consecration to right. Before us is liberty more glorious than even the fathers conceived, and an application of the laws of justice more sympathetic and comprehensive than the world has yet witnessed. Toward that, and not to the past, turn we our faces. "I think the soul to be nothing but light," said Mrs. Hutchinson. The light is exhaustless. May it with endless shining break forth in the faith and the works of this ancient church!

[1] Sketch of Quincy, p. 275; History of Norfolk Co.

II.

THE CHURCH OF STATESMEN.

THE GLORY OF THIS LATTER HOUSE SHALL BE GREATER THAN THAT OF THE FORMER, SAITH THE LORD OF HOSTS: AND IN THIS PLACE WILL I GIVE PEACE, SAITH THE LORD OF HOSTS. — *Haggai* ii. 9.

THE sermon preached last Sunday was intended to set before you the exciting events which preceded the "embodying" of this church, and so was a preparation for the interesting commemorative exercises in which we are this day to take part. You will remember that for exactly one year, — that is, from November, 1636, to November, 1637, — the Rev. John Wheelwright labored with the "Chappel of Ease" which was gathered in this place. Then when Wheelwright and his friends were banished, and many others had gone with them into voluntary exile, it was as though no band of worshippers had ever come together here to listen to the "Word" and to join in singing the sacred psalms. The church at the Mount was effectually abolished. And we hear nothing of a concerted movement to gather again a church till the 16th of September, 1639. For a year and ten months no sufficient number of the inhabitants felt enough in heart to attempt a new organization. The natural leaders of the people were gone, and those of the liberal party who remained were sullen and resentful.

It is not to be supposed, however, that there was entire stagnation at the Mount. During this time there was a great shifting of population and a great change in the proprietorship of lands. The banished and the exiled were selling their estates as rapidly as they could to those pressing this way from Boston and from over sea. Coddington's lands were bought at a bargain by Capt. William Tyng, a Boston merchant, who sold them over again; and John Wheelwright disposed of his " great possessions " at a sacrifice we may well believe. But the new influx mingling with the " remnant " infused into the settlement a more vigorous life. These later immigrants, some of whom most likely were passengers in " the great store of ships " which arrived at Boston in 1638, had no vital interest in the recent controversy, and were prepared to go forward in the course usual with prospering plantations.

FIRST CHURCH GATHERED.

So on Monday, the 16th day of September, 1639, the inhabitants of the Mount assembled to enter solemnly into new church relations.[1] The enterprise, however, has

[1] The Rev. Mr. Hancock in his sermons preached "Sept. 16, 1739, on completing the first century since the gathering of " the First Church, is very careful to state explicitly several times that our fathers were "embodied in a church-state here this day an hundred years ago." Then in a note he furthermore says, " The church was gathered on Monday, Sept. 16, 1639." It is some confirmation of this, were it needed, that " Sept. 16, 1639, was Monday," as Dr. George E. Ellis assures me. When Mr. Hancock wrote his sermons he had in his possession our oldest book of records, now lost. After amending a later record by writing "16" where some one had written "Sept. 17," he gives a short account of the renewal of the covenant at the centennial anniversary

a look as though it were suddenly conceived, as though indeed it had been talked over "after meeting" in Boston the day before, and that then on the spur of the moment ministers Tompson and Flynt had come to the determination that the almost shepherdless sheep of this pasture should forthwith be more conveniently provided for. These two ministers were peculiarly fitted to organize a church here. Mr. William Tompson was then a recent arrival in the colony. He shared none of the bitterness toward liberals which had been harbored by his brother ministers in the antinomian conflict, and was prepared to act the pacificator in a kindly and charitable spirit. His companion, Mr. Henry Flynt, was by disposition and open confession even more delicately adapted to the situation. He was himself of the liberal party, and at that very time was under censure for signing the petition in behalf of Wheelwright. It was at the call of such sympathetic leadership that the inhabitants of the Mount came together once more to form a church of their own. They were all there, men and women, their profound interest in the occasion appearing in their solemn deportment and subdued conversation. But not many of them then entered into church relations. Seven had come to be considered about the proper number with which to begin a church. And so only six, with the two ministers, actively participated in the important work. These six, — George Rose, Stephen Kinsley, John Dassett, William

"on September 16th, being the Lord's day, 1739," ending with these words: "See Ch. Covt. among ye Records of this Church." That covenant now exists only in the copy he printed with his centennial discourses. Add ten days to change from old to new style would make September 26 the proper date of our anniversary.

Potter, Martin Saunders the tavern-keeper, and Gregory Belcher, — new men mostly and small farmers, separated themselves from the rest of the congregation as those on the whole most free in their conscience and best fitted by their orthodoxy to begin so weighty a business. Then, as was the fashion, they confessed their sins one to another, made profession of their faith, were consecrated by prayer, and in right brotherly way stood up before the assembly and gave one another in solemn covenant the hand of fellowship.

After this manner was the church founded. It should have been an occasion of pious gladness, but there is to be detected running through the proceedings a feeling of constraint. In the covenant not only do they designate themselves by such usual phrases as " poor unworthy creatures," but they seem really troubled about " all the remnants of anti-Christian pollution wherein sometimes we have walked." They were trying, some of them, to be properly sorry for their heresies, and to feel a due amount of contrition. This was notably the case with minister Flynt, who could not be brought to acknowledge his error till some eight months later than this. Without doubt there were many in that assembly who, like him, were straining their conscience to conclude they had been in the wrong, and to bring themselves into agreement with the prevailing theology. These were in sufficient numbers, notwithstanding recent additions, to give tone to the proceedings and character to the new-formed church. It was in their minds, also, that the loss of their chief men was a sad blow to the prosperity of the settlement. Winthrop unconsciously draws attention to this.

He and others, when it was first proposed to establish an independent church at the Mount, were loath to give any encouragement because so many "chief men" would be withdrawn from Boston. Now, in writing of the founding of our church in this September of 1639, he puts down not a word about "chief men," but only that "many poor men" petitioned to have a church. What is done at the Mount is of so little concern now to Boston that Winthrop does not remember accurately the day when the church was gathered, nor the day when Tompson was ordained.

FIRST MINISTERS AND DEACONS.

Accepting the Rev. John Hancock for best authority (he was very careful what he wrote, and had before him Teacher Flynt's record), we find that Tompson was ordained pastor eight days after the church was gathered; that is, Tuesday, the 24th of September, 1639. Who the elders officiating at this ordination were we do not know; but whoever they were they would not at the same time ordain Henry Flynt as teacher. He had not made his submission yet. But the grave, conscientious young man (he was now about thirty-two years old) at last avowed that he would petition to have his name blotted out from the paper written in defence of Wheelwright; and so, on the 17th of March following, he too was set over this church as one of its ministers. His petition was granted by the court the same day — May 13, 1640 — it granted the inhabitants of the Mount liberty to incorporate themselves as the town of Braintree. I cannot but think it was similarity of belief which drew Henry Flynt to the Mount. He was still liberal for all his recantation; the broad mind and the tolerant spirit were there, however pious his submission. Thus the church continued to be an undogmatic, a progressive congregation, with one minister, at least, entirely sympathetic. Evidence of this I seem to see in the first choice for deacon of Samuel Bass, who had been fined five pounds "for contempt" about the time of the banishment of Wheelwright;[1] in "the desire of the church of Christ at Mount Wollaston that Alexander Winchester,"[2] Mr. Vane's man, be dismissed from Boston church for their help also in the office of deacon; and in the fact that some of Mount Wollaston continued to "receive" at Boston, as though affairs here were not entirely satisfactory to them.[3] Mr. Tompson may have been just as liberal-minded as his colleague, but I speak especially of Mr. Flynt because he sustained a closer and more constant relation with our church. The country generally seemed to conclude that one minister was enough for us, and made three several attempts to divert our pastor to other duties. The ministers of the colony, in prayerful session, selected him and another to journey to Virginia and supply the means of grace to such as could not find it in the ministrations of the Church of England. He preached with power and influenced many; but the "Old Dominion" soon

---

[1] Records of the General Court, Dec. 4, 1638.
[2] Boston First Church Records, July 12, 1640.
[3] Lechford's Plaine Dealing, p. 41, and note by J. H. Trumbull.

drove him out, being as intolerant of Puritans as
Massachusetts was of Episcopalians. It might be interesting
to speculate upon the probable course of the
history of Virginia if the independency and moral earnestness
of the New England churches had obtained at
that time a strong and permanent hold upon the hearts of
the people there. But I must not be tempted aside; I
would only interject the remark that thus early Braintree
began to regard Southern affairs. Hardly had
Tompson returned from this missionary journey when
he was chosen to accompany the army in the threatened
war with the Narragansetts. He was to blow a
silver trumpet before the host, and preach the word to
them. Of "tall, comely presence," quite military looking,
and also quite brave and obedient to all calls of
duty, he would have acquitted himself well. But the
war did not break out, and he returned to his pastoral
charge. Then in 1648 he was invited to settle over
the church Wheelwright had founded in Exeter, N. H.
That gentleman, fearing the advancing power of the
Massachusetts government, had fled to Wells. The offer
made to Tompson was liberal, — thirty pounds a year,
the profits of the town saw-mill, and the use of the
house and land bought of Wheelwright. But Tompson
resisted the temptation. What led those of Exeter,
one wonders, to send for Tompson? Was it because
of what friends here wrote to the former dwellers at
the Mount there? Did they recommend him as a worthy
successor of Wheelwright? We can only guess;
at all events, the church in Braintree prospered under
the ministration of its pastor and teacher, and all its

aspirations, liberal or other, seemed satisfied. These ministers passed away, — Tompson in 1666, Flynt in 1668, — leaving behind them the sweet remembrance of their gravity, integrity, purity, and holiness. Of their wives the least to be said is that they bequeathed to this parish the names Abigail and Dorothy, which since have been so highly honored.

STILL "THE SOUR LEVEN OF THOSE SINFUL OPINIONS."

A liberal party vigorously manifested itself in the choice for successors of its first ministers. This party was for calling the Rev. Josiah Flynt, son of their late lamented teacher. Opposition was made on the ground that the candidate had uttered "divers dangerous heterodoxies, delivered, and that without caution, in his public preaching." Many meetings were had about it, with "very uncomfortable debates" and "awful divisions." The liberals so far prevailed as to elect Mr. Flynt and a Mr. Bulkeley; but as the ballot was not single and the quarrelling had been bitter, neither would accept, and for four years the distracted church continued without a settled minister. "The disorders among us," wrote one of our members on a subsequent occasion, "call for tears and lamentations, rather than to be remembered." This is very true; and they are mentioned now only to make it plain that in this early period of our church's history there was no lack of mental vigor and the manifestation of an independent spirit. The very earnestness of the dispute and its long continuance is evidence that these forefathers of ours had strong convictions. Their religion was a vital thing to them, and entirely possessed their hearts and minds. Characteristic of the church from the earliest times has been its stubborn strength, its faithfulness to its ideals, its self-reliance, its almost rude directness. These founders of our town were no lovers of smooth words and compromises. "Poor men" they might be in estate, but without question they were rich in mental power and tenacious moral strength. They stand forth as marked examples of the plain, blunt, serious, conscientious English Puritan, of the tolerant Miltonic sort, sure of his ground, vigorous in the defence of it, yet with face toward the larger view and broader principle. And in the history of this church, almost typical in its natural gradations, is the development of religious belief and moral conviction through wider statements and more liberal tendencies.

THE FIRST MEETING-HOUSE DESCRIBED.

The scene of these earlier religious adjustments was the first meeting-house built by the settlers, the square stone structure which was situated in the middle of what is now Hancock Street, a little to the north of its junction with Canal Street. There, on the tongue of land which rose above the Town River swamps to the east and west of it, the little building was conspicuous. I imagine it was in shape like the old Hingham church,— a platform rising from the apex of the roof, on which at a later day swung a bell. Near the church, and erected almost as early, were the schoolhouse and the tavern, institutions having effects how opposite! This place was indeed the town centre, with its little square, or common. The main road from Plymouth to Boston ran through it, dividing when it came to the meeting-house, passing by each end of it and uniting again just above the "meeting-house bridge" over the Town-River. The Webb house in which Mr. Jones now lives in the "hollow" is the only one left of those which formerly stood near the meeting-house in the town square. It was certainly built before the year 1700, it may even have been occupied by Parson Tompson, and faced toward the square on the line of the road as it diverged to the eastward to go around the meeting-house.

The church was entered by a door at the east end, and very likely by another at the west end. The pulpit, as I conjecture, was situated against the south wall, and on either side of it running entirely around the building were galleries. In front of the pulpit were the deacons' seats, where Samuel Bass, Richard Brackett, Benjamin Saville, and other worthies "held out the box" to receive the regular Sunday contribution as the congregation flocked up and filed past. The seats for the worshippers were at first plain, rude benches in two rows, — the women occupying one row, the men the other. There was also the women's gallery and the men's gallery. The "seating the meeting-house," — that is, the assigning to persons the sixteen or eighteen inches of plank they were to occupy for the year, — was always a delicate task, and sometimes occasioned heart-burnings. Social rank and moral worth and age were generally considered, but money could not buy the best places as now. Free seats and a certain equality before the Lord was the accepted rule. The pew system was introduced the 15th of January, 1700 (to be precise). Then Capt. John Wilson was granted liberty to make a pew in some convenient place. He built his little pen in the back part of the meeting-house against the wall; then Minister Fiske built his by the east window; next, Col. Edmund Quincy built his by the side of Mr. Wilson's. And so they added pew to pew, till the walls of the church all around were possessed by them. Only one part of the walls had neither gallery nor pew against it. This was the space above the pulpit. Then it was voted (I think it is with regard to this earliest church) that a certain prominent personage "might build him a pew over the pulpit, provided he so builds as not to darken the pulpit." The late Josiah Quincy, in quoting this vote, wrote, —

"A friend of mine here suggests that, as a figure of speech, pews may now be said to be built over the pulpit with some frequency, and regrets that the good divines of the town, whose life-long sway was arbitrary and unquestioned, did not have the wit to prevent that perilous permission. For notwithstanding the wholesome caution of the old record, it has been found impossible 'not to darken the pulpit' when the pews are placed above it."

Let the picture of that diminutive stone meeting-house, as I have outlined it, take form in your minds. Imagine it filled with your ancestors, with those whose dust sanctifies the little cemetery yonder, the memory of whose sterling virtues is to us a sacred possession. How plain the interior! — no color, no art, no large breadths of space; a place rude in its simplicity. And how devoid of art, also, the Sunday's service! — a long prayer, a long sermon, and the psalms slowly lined out, and sung tunelessly almost.[1] Yet how serious the faces of the worshippers; how lit up with strong, noble reverence! Along the fore-seats sat the oldest among them. "I shall never forget," wrote John Adams of a period later than this, "the rows of venerable heads ranged along those front benches which, as a young fellow, I used to gaze upon." They bowed, all of them, — young and old together, — before the Lord, and the thought of His presence made their poor surroundings glorious. How changed their attitude, however, during those stormy meetings when "some were for Paul and some for Apollos"! Lieut. Edmund Quincy presiding in the little pulpit is hardly able to keep the excited gathering in order. A vigorous speaker will not have "heterodox" Flynt on any account, and his words are greeted with ready applause by some others like-minded. Captain Brackett and Deacon Bass and Goodman Faxon are all up at once, uttering themselves in defence of the right of a man to think for himself, and on the importance of personal righteousness. And so the battle goes on, and by it the Lord's work is done as effectually as in the Sunday worship. Truth emerges from the tumult, and peace attends upon the more rational convictions. There is no such trouble again, no "awful divisions" over charges of "heterodoxy." The liberalizing element, potent in the forming of the church, is

---

[1] As late as "May 26, 1723, Major Quincy was fairly and clearly chosen by written votes to the office of tuning the Psalm in our assemblies for public worship."—"1761, March 29, Voted to sing Dr. Watts's hymns and spiritual songs on Sacramental occasions."

potent still, and the congregation as a body drifts complacently away from the stern continent of Calvinistic doctrine. When next there is earnest discussion of dogma, it is manifest that virtually the entire congregation is with the minister in his most liberal and independent ideas.

In the period we are now considering, the congregation eventually so "moderated their spirits" that they acquiesced when the County Court in November, 1671, interfered, where so many other means had failed, and sent "Mr. Moses Fiske to improve his labors in preaching the word at Braintry, until the church there agree to obtain supply." This proved a quite fortunate assumption, as at the close of his first Sunday of service "about twenty of the brethren came to visit at Mr. Flynt's, manifesting in the name of the church their ready acceptance of what the court had done;" and two months later "the church, by their messengers," as Mr. Fiske records, "did jointly and unanimously desire my settlement amongst them. . . . The day of my solemn espousals to this church and congregation" was the 11th of September, 1672. He was then thirty years old, and for a period of thirty-six years "was zealously diligent for God and the good of men, — one who thought no labor, cost, or suffering too dear a price for the good of his people."

A CONGREGATION FORMED AT THE "SOUTH END."

It was during his pastorate that the town was divided into the north and south precincts. Not without calling "forth a great deal of human nature" was this accomplished. Those who lived far away in the south part of the town were becoming painfully conscious that it was a long distance to "meeting, and through such bad ways, whereby the Lord's day, which is a day of rest, was to them a day of labor rather." Reasonably enough, they asked that a new and larger edifice be built at a point more central. The old stone meeting-house was at this time much out of repair, and very plainly also it could not adequately accommodate the growing parish. Accordingly, at a town-meeting in 1695 it was "voted that a new meeting-house should be erected." "This," writes Mr. C. F. Adams the younger, "did not meet the views of old Col. Edmund Quincy and others who lived in the northern limits; consequently they went to work to prevent anything being done at all, and at a private meeting held at Colonel Quincy's they 'did agree among themselves to shingle the old house, pretending to be at the whole charge themselves.' But, none the less, 'several pounds were afterwards gathered by a rate upon the whole town.'" Then they of the south began to talk about organizing a separate church. This project was also opposed, on the ground that the burden of paying Minister Fiske his eighty or ninety pounds a year would fall upon a reduced number in the north. So north and south had "much sinful discourse" between them, and "some misapprehension about church discipline." However, on the second day of May, 1706, the frame of a new meeting-house was raised in the south part of the town; and at a town-meeting the next November it was voted, as gracefully as the circumstances would permit, "that as there were two meeting-houses erected in this town, the south end shall be a congregation by themselves." On the 10th of September, 1707, the Rev. Hugh Adams was ordained pastor of the South Church; but the contention over finances was only ended with the death of Mr. Fiske, Aug. 10, 1708.

ADJUSTMENT WITH THE CHURCH OF ENGLAND.

During the ministry of Mr. Fiske his congregation was also agitated over the appearance in town of the Church of England. How these "prelatists" got established in this Puritan settlement, whether by immigration or by conversion of degenerate Congregationalists, it would be interesting to ascertain. We know that in Boston a few early appeared in the train of the king's officers, and that with the advent of Andros in 1686 that town was forced to adjust itself to regular assemblies of the hated worship. Next to residents of Boston, the people here were first among Congregationalists to be called upon to solve the problem of how to live with the church which numbered the "martyr king" — Charles I. — with the saints, and named all the leaders of the Puritan revolution as "violent and bloodthirsty men." It was a question bristling with animosities. The English Church was then foreign to our soil and unrecognized by law, yet it claimed the king's colonies for the prayer-book and the prelacy. A member of that Church, asking assistance for his fellow-worshippers here, wrote in 1702: "Brantry should be minded; it is in the heart of New England, and a learned and sober man would do great good and encourage the other towns to desire the like. If the Church can be settled in New England it pulls up schisms in America by the root, that being the fountain that supplies, with infectious streams, the rest of America." The schismatics of "Brantry" were not at all eager to be pulled up. On the contrary, they were rather strongly inclined to do some uprooting themselves. However, in spite of their longings they really did treat the members of the Church of England handsomely. According to Puritan law, these prelatists as well as all others were taxed for the support of the Puritan churches, and were required to attend the stated meetings of them when they had no services of their own. But how charitably this church dealt with them let the Rev. John Hancock tell: —

"I verily think the conduct of this church and congregation towards our brethren of the Church of England has been Christian and exemplary. I will mention several instances of it to the glory of God and their praise. In the vacancy before the Rev. Mr. Miller received holy orders for this place, this church admitted to their communion all such members of the Church of England as desired to have occasional communion with us, and allowed them what posture of devotion they pleased, and they used to receive the sacrament standing. . . . This parish, upon Mr. Miller's coming, reimbursed to the declared members of the Church of England their proportion of the charge of my settlement, and generously excused them from any further payments towards my support."

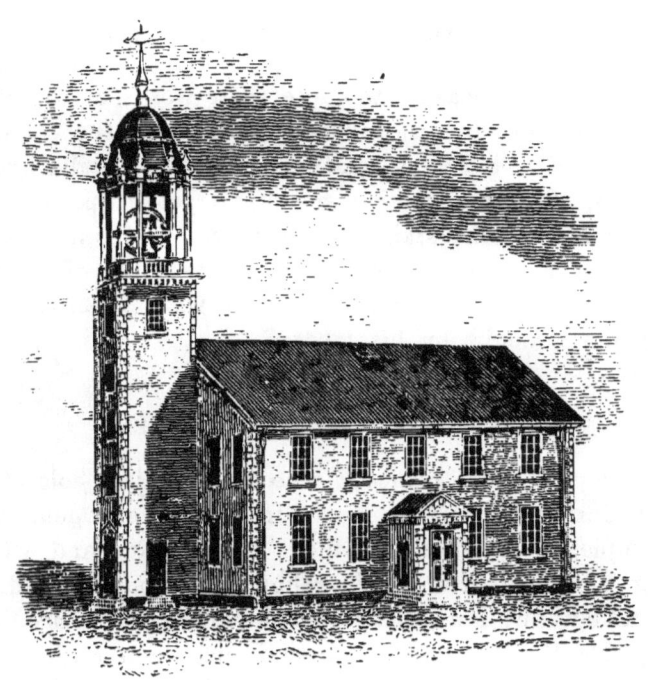

HANCOCK'S MEETING-HOUSE, AS ALTERED IN 1805.

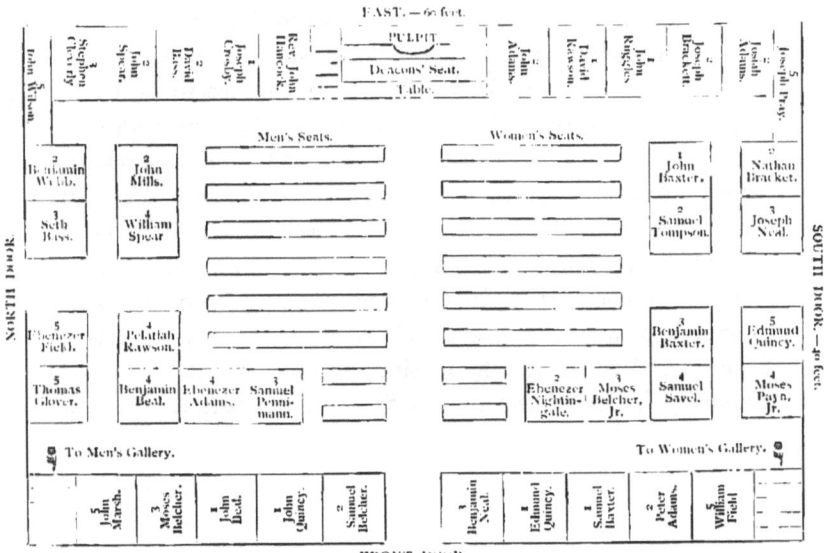

Ground Floor as it was when Church was dedicated in 1732. Numbers indicate valuation lots, — "Lot 1, eight pews, at £25; lot 2, twelve, at £15 each," etc.

It gives me pleasure to quote these words of the Rev. Mr. Hancock, for they clearly testify to the tolerant spirit which even at that early day prevailed here. Indeed, we can say that no single act of persecution for opinion's sake stains our history. Is this not owing in some measure to the words and example of Wheelwright; to the inclination toward what is broad and humane wrought by his labors?

MEETING-HOUSES LESS THAN MEN.

This same Mr. Hancock who thus praises toleration and Christian courtesy, was himself an exponent and example of brotherly kindness and charity and whatever is most substantial in religion. In our chronology he follows the faithful Joseph Marsh, who was installed May 18, 1709, and in a spiritual succession ranks with the best of our ministers. Ordained May 2, 1726, he was the last pastor to lead the devotions of this church in the old meeting-house. Its leaks and fissures admitting in winter's storms cartloads of snow, were no more to be "repaired." A new church was at last to be built. The site first proposed was "at Colonel Quincy's gate;" then where the old meeting-house stood; but it was decided eventually to place it "at the ten milestone, or near unto it." This was exactly fixed "on the training-field" a little to the south of the "ten milestone."

Mr. Hancock thought the compassing a new house of worship was the great achievement of his ministry. When he records its dedication, Oct. 8, 1732, he spontaneously breaks forth into praises in the sonorous Latin speech. As it stood there on the training-field, fair and beautiful in his eyes, he felt it to be a glorious monument of the energy of his people, destined to win for them great respect and influence. But however notable that event, its influence in shaping the destiny and establishing the character of this society was as nothing compared with two other happenings seemingly ordinary enough. These two items stand in his record of baptisms: "John, son of John Adams, Oct. 26, 1735," and "John Hancock, my son, Jan. 16, 1736-7." Proud as a father, no doubt, he was on the latter occasion; but proud for his church he might well have been on both occasions. The son of the deacon and the son of the minister were to bring more fame to First Church and add more to its character and influence than any temple of wood or stone, however spacious and costly. How true it is that evermore it is not the material environment but the spirit which emanates from man or God, — the truth, the patriotism, the faith, the integrity, — which establishes the fame of all institutions, and makes effectual all the noble power of them! Heretofore, through many years, children of this church had become notable. The Quincy family especially, in every generation since the first Edmund came from England in 1633, had given to the country magistrates, military officers, representatives, judges. The church had a share in their fame and the unfailing assistance of their wealth and wisdom. Now with these were to be enrolled John Hancock, the liberal patriot and honorable Governor, and John Adams, the Puritan statesman of the Revolution, anticipating Independence with Puri-

tan conscience, and advocating it with Puritan persistence; the Chief Magistrate —

> "Of soul sincere,
> In action faithful and in honor clear;
> Who broke no promise, served no private end."

He was such a man as the best traditions and great principles of our early New England life tended to make. This church proudly claims him; perceives his original mental force, his moral independence and fervor, to be consonant with its centuries of teaching.

"ON FAME'S ETERNALL BEAD-ROLL."

How many other statesmen, all after this same order, have been born to us! From the unbroken and ascending line of the Quincys still have issued men prominent in public life who belonged to us, though baptized, it may be, in the metropolis which with this place they honored as their home. John Quincy, one of the most active men in colonial affairs, for many years Speaker of the House and Colonel of the Suffolk Regiment, was a life-long member of this church, and for a quarter of a century or more the favorite presiding officer of parish meetings. And who so constant an attendant upon the services of this church, all through the long months of his summer sojourn among us, as "Boston's Great Mayor" and representative to Congress, Josiah Quincy? His tall manly form and reverent aspect are still clear in the minds of many of this congregation. Other public and notable men you will call to remembrance, — Thomas Greenleaf, Richard Cranch, — yet I must not stop to name them, but hurry on to speak of him, the son of a President and President himself, whose character and achievements are of that high moral and intellectual order which in any age would render him illustrious. For record of his earliest connection with this church I resort again to the time-worn annals of the ministers. This time the writing is that of old Parson Wibird, and under the headline "Baptisms, 1767," reads, "Jn? Quincy, S. Jn? Adams, July 12." The child John Quincy Adams, schooled and trained into manhood in a remarkably practical and liberal fashion, shows himself more essentially a Puritan than even his father. His piety, his devotion to truth and right, his indomitable will, all mark him as a genuine descendant of those who surrendered all to live in accord with the spiritual intent and spiritual principles of the universe. The broad New England church in the world of affairs never had truer representative. His high aims, and methods as high, exalted the office of President; and later he was the "old man eloquent," whose voice to his last hour rang clear and unfaltering in defence of liberty and human rights. For all his great renown and high public station, his name is frequently to be met with in our church records on committees appointed to represent the congregation at Unitarian conventions and installations of ministers. Entirely one with this society in spirit, he also identified himself with its practical administrations.

And still the line stretches out with no abatement in mental ability or moral force. His son, Charles Francis Adams, so lately gathered to his fathers and mourned by a nation which appreciates in constantly increasing degree

I am
Your most Obedt
John Hancock

his fine and forceful character and measureless services, was a statesman by birth and acquirements. Every public position to which he was elevated he honored; and we do not need to remind you how as Minister to England during the war for the Union his clear intelligence and resolute moral strength prevented battles, converted a formidable foe to a friend, and in calm diplomatic councils did as much to preserve this nation as did Grant in the rough open field of war. This great man also belongs to us; proudly we claim him as we claim his fathers, — ours by blood and preference. "He loved to come here. He loved to frequent the house of God always. It was his never-failing weekly resort. Religion was not merely the daily practice of his home, — it was the centre of his life." [1]

But I have said enough; more than is needful I have named of those "on Fame's eternall bead-roll," to demonstrate the distinctive character of this church among even New England churches. It is THE CHURCH OF STATESMEN, — every man of them (it is the luminous fact to be cherished) magnanimous, sincere, and genuine, and illustrating in the face of the world the eternal principles of the Christian religion here taught and reverenced. To their influence and fame it is owing that this church is known throughout the land, and that pilgrimages are made to it. To their influence, do I say? But not to theirs alone. Who can resist the thought that its virtuous and noble women, — Mrs. Abigail Adams, Mrs. John Quincy Adams, Mrs. Charles Francis Adams, Miss

---

[1] Dr. William Everett, "Address in Commemoration of the Life and Services of Charles Francis Adams."

Eliza Susan Quincy, — add a graciousness to that distinction and make it entirely beautiful in character?

This peculiarity of our church has a recognition of long standing. Josiah Quincy, in his "Figures of the Past," writes, —

"An air of respectful deference to John Adams seemed to pervade the building. The ministers brought their best sermons when they came to exchange, and had a certain consciousness in their manner as if officiating before royalty. The medley of stringed and wind instruments in the gallery, — a survival of the sacred trumpets and shaums mentioned by King David, — seemed to the imagination of a child to be making discord together in honor of the venerable chief who was the centre of interest."

But however admired and reverenced, these great men were still Puritans in their simplicity and entire submission to the Highest. They venerated their little village church and its worship. Called by their official duties to sojourn in the great cities of Europe, they were witnesses of the pageantry of courts in which no ceremony was left out; they mingled with the brilliant concourse which thronged the gay *salons;* they listened to the majestic harmonies in the magnificent cathedrals of England and the Continent, — and yet they returned with content, and with an even increased devotion, to the plain ordinances and unadorned principles of their fathers. In their loyalty, as well as their fame, they honored the Church of Christ in this place. When travelling in Spain, John Adams forbore to bow before a shrine reverently shown him, containing some sacred relics. The shocked custodian inquired in French of the archbishop who was doing

Josiah Quincy

the honors of the occasion, "Is not the gentleman a Christian?" "Yes," answered the prelate, "in his own way." These honored men of our communion, whatever the place they were in, or the pomp by which they were surrounded, were Christians in their own way, — the way they were taught here in this church and

> "At that best academe, a mother's knee."

FIRST CHURCH PROGRESSIVE STILL.

It might easily be taken for granted that a church which nurtured men and women so thoughtful and broadly intelligent would dispense no narrow belief; and, in truth, the slightest investigation shows that in this regard it was singular among even New England churches. The liberal spirit so early interfused appears in the utterance of every one of its greatest preachers. The sermons of the Rev. John Hancock written to commemorate the close of the first century of our church's history, are remarkable for what he deliberately does not say. In them there is entire absence of Calvinistic dogma. Already the cruder phases of Puritanism had been discarded. It was during his ministry, too, that "some persons of a sober life and good conversation signified their unwillingness to join in full communion with the church, unless they may be admitted to it without making a public relation of their spiritual experiences, which (they say) the church has no warrant in the word of God to require." So a "great majority" voted they would not "any more insist upon the making a relation as a necessary form of full communion." But it is when we come to the Rev. Lemuel Briant that we find liberalism self-conscious and aggressive. This minister, a young man of twenty-four when he succeeded Mr. Hancock in the September of 1745, is characterized as intellectually a remarkable man. Certainly he was as writer and preacher brilliant, incisive, independent, and possessing little regard for conventionalities. "Had he lived he might have held his ground, and succeeded in advancing by one long stride the tardy progress of liberal Christianity in Massachusetts." He neglected to teach the children of his parish the catechism, preferring plain Scripture; he was guilty, said his opponents, of "the absurdity and blasphemy of substituting the personal righteousness of men in the room of the surety-righteousness of Christ;" he praised moral virtue; he protested against such interpretation of the Bible as affronted human reason. For this he was called "Socinian" and "Armenian," and a council of sister churches was summoned to try him. With an independence almost unheard of, he slighted the council and would not go near it. But as it declared there existed grounds for the complaints against him, a committee of his own church was appointed to consider the matter. Col. John Quincy was at the head of this committee, and it reported a series of resolutions which may fairly be regarded as remarkable for the times. They were adopted by almost the entire church, the few "aggrieved brethren" seeming to be quite pacified. In these resolutions the people defended their pastor's use of "pure Scripture" instead of the catechism; and they honored the right of private judgment, commending "Mr. Briant for the pains he took to pro-

JOHN GUIN
F. S.
AGED

LOUISA CATHERINE ADAMS,
(Mrs. J. Q. Adams.)
1795.
AGED 21.

mote a free and impartial examination into all articles of our holy religion, so that all may judge even of themselves what is right."

Upon such broad foundation this church placed itself seventy years before Channing preached the famous Baltimore sermon, which precipitated the separation of the Unitarian churches from the main body of Congregationalists. In principle it was a Unitarian church long before the liberal aspirations of New England had taken definite shape and name. To this John Adams gives his testimony. He was a growing lad during the controversy over the beliefs of Mr. Briant, and its effect upon himself was manifest in his rejection of the ministry as a profession; as he wrote, "the reason of my quitting the divinity was my opinion concerning some disputed points." Through all the phases of a developing liberal Christianity he with vigorous thinking then passed, and many fellow-parishioners with him; so that in 1815, when at last the Unitarian outbreak occurred, he could write as follows to Dr. Morse of Charlestown, who had sent him a pamphlet setting forth the new opinions: —

"I thank you for your favor of the 10th and the pamphlet enclosed, entitled 'American Unitarianism.' I have turned over its leaves and find nothing that was not familiarly known to me. In the preface, Unitarianism is represented as only thirty years old in New England. I can testify as a witness to its old age. Sixty-five years ago my own minister, the Rev. Lemuel Briant, Dr. Jonathan Mayhew of the West Church in Boston, the Rev. Mr. Steele of Hingham, the Rev. John Brown of Cohasset, and perhaps equal to all, if not above all, the Rev. Mr. Gay of Hingham, were Unitarians. Among the laity how many could I name, — lawyers, physicians, tradesmen, farmers! But at present I will name only one, — Richard Cranch, a man who had studied divinity, and Jewish and Christian antiquities, more than any clergyman now existing in New England."

The minister who followed Mr. Briant may have been as liberal, but he was not at all aggressive in his religious or other opinions.[1] In the company of the Rev. Anthony Wibird "something is to be learned of human nature, human life, love, courtship, marriage," wrote the stirring and ambitious John Adams at twenty-two; " but his opinion out " of these things " is not very valuable. His soul is lost in a dronish effeminacy." Somewhat later in 1775, Boston then being besieged by the patriots, Abigail Adams wrote to her husband, " I could not bear to hear our inanimate old bachelor. Mrs. Cranch and I took our chaise and went to hear Mr. Haven of Dedham; and we had no occasion to repent our eleven miles ride." But however the " inanimate old bachelor " whose opinions were chiefly valuable as they regarded " courtship and marriage " might drone away, his church continued to expand in thought and to gain clearer conceptions of " moral virtue." In a marked degree it was a church whose power was in its pews, and thus a good example of

[1] 1755, Feb. 5. We went to Braintree, joined in the ordination Council. Mr. Wibird the candidate, having (upon examination of his principles, particularly about the Deity of Christ, the satisfaction he made to the justice of God for the sins of men, original sin, and the influence of the spirit of God, and our justifying righteousness before God) given satisfaction to the Council, they voted to proceed to his ordination. Rev. Mr. Langdon of Portsmouth began with prayer; Rev. Mr. Appleton, who was chosen member of the Council upon the venerable Mr. Niles declining it, preached from Levi. x. 3. The Rev. Mr. Gay of Hingham being chosen upon Mr. Niles declining it, gave the charge; and I being chosen gave the right hand of fellowship. — *MSS. Record of Rev. Mr. Dunbar of Stoughton, now Canton.*

worshippers after the Congregational order, — a society of "the brethren." In diaries and records one discerns how alive are these farmers, lawyers, and physicians to facts and principles of real religion; how keen for moral distinctions, how impatient of cant. So through the forty-five years during which Parson Wibird preached (a man "withal of great dignity, and beloved and respected by his people," as the Rev. Peter Whitney testifies), the church slowly drifted onward upon the stream of rational religion toward a world of higher thoughts and nobler aspirations.

"AS IT IS TO THIS DAY."

By the time Peter Whitney was ordained, the 5th of February, 1800, the church was fairly set in this direction, and had no changes to make, no controversy to disturb it, when Channing's sermon forced the congregations of New England to take sides. Good, kind, pleasant-spoken Peter Whitney, — there are men and women with us still who remember him well, who were baptized by him, even married by him. They like to tell of his genial humor and plain human ways. The great event of his ministry was the dedication of the "Stone Temple" on the twelfth day of November, 1828. By the munificence of John Adams and the encouragement of his son John Quincy Adams was this temple erected "for the public worship of God, and for public instruction in the doctrines and duties of the Christian religion." With its marble tablets and tomb, "durable as the rocks of their native town," it has become a notable monument to their services and character.

On the 3d day of June, 1835, the Rev. William Parsons Lunt was installed as colleague with Mr. Whitney. A melancholy interest attaches to his name, partly on account of his pensive and earnest character, but most because of his untimely death far from home and friends while travelling in the Holy Land.

> "But oh that the thoughtful scholar, —
> His mind at its fullest noon, —
> That the preacher's tongue
> And the poet's song
> Should pass away so soon!"

In the sands of Arabian Akaba his dust was interred, — how distant from the "tombs of the prophets," his predecessors, in our burial-place which he was so careful to preserve! Dr. Lunt, always meditating upon the highest themes, led his people still on where reason joined with reverence showed the way. Famed for scholarship and poetic gifts, he is ranked among the ablest of the ministers of the First Church. His discourse delivered at the interment of his venerated parishioner John Quincy Adams, is "worthy of a place by the side of any funeral oration of ancient or modern times," and his two discourses written for the Two Hundredth Anniversary of this church are remarkable for careful statement, extensive research, and perspicuity of style. By these and other productions of his pen he obtained great renown.

Mr. John D. Wells was ordained Dr. Lunt's successor the 27th of December, 1860. Coming here just on the eve of the great Civil War, Mr. Wells threw himself with passionate devotion upon the side of the Union, and not only inspired his parishioners with patriotic feelings, but himself enlisted and led the way where actions more eloquently spoke. Received with hearty welcome when he returned from the front, he once more took up his duties among you, and with entire faithfulness performed them till failing health obliged him to resign. Your manifest affection for him is greater praise than I may presume to render.

For four years before my own installation you were without a settled pastor. During that time you listened to many preachers. A few of them cannot but be mentioned, — such as Dr. William Everett, whose presence with us this day is denied us owing to his severe illness; Dr. A. P. Putnam, who occupied this pulpit for several months, and who was invited to remain here permanently; and the Rev. E. C. Butler, who twice was urged to become the minister of this parish.

Finally, on the 24th of March, 1880, I was installed your minister. I hardly dare confess how hard it has been to rightly labor with a "plentiful lack" of self-confidence, and how poor the labor seems for the most part, now at the end of ten years. But you have continued your activities, dispensing a constant charity, manifesting an unfailing interest in the advancement of pure Christianity and moral reforms. Many, very many have passed away from among us; yet we have grown, and the promise of the future is inspiring.

The most memorable event which has occurred among you since I have been your minister was the ending of the earthly existence of our great fellow-worshipper, the Hon. Charles Francis Adams. On Tuesday the 23d of November, 1886, this church was opened to receive his remains, and after the solemn and simple service befitting the occasion, they were borne hence to be interred in the soil he loved so well. Again for a high and solemn purpose was the church opened the 4th of July, 1887, when Dr. William Everett delivered his noble address in commemoration of the life and services of Mr. Adams. Mrs. Adams did not long survive her husband; she too passed away full of years and beloved by all. Another notable event which may be mentioned is the erection and dedication of our chapel a year ago; and perhaps it is also worthy of record that at last this is not the only Unitarian church within the limits of the ancient town of Braintree. October 23, 1887, the present flourishing Unitarian society at Wollaston, under the charge of the Rev. W. S. Key, was started; and for a year or more the Rev. J. F. Moors, D. D., has been preaching to a very vigorous congregation of our faith in Randolph.

"THE CONCLUSION OF THE WHOLE MATTER."

In this pleasant anniversary celebration our interest chiefly has been with the past. We have sought to understand the vanished times, and make the people of them live once more. During these last months, while thus looking backward, passing strange to me has seemed this show of things. Gone are all those sons of men who here toiled and fretted, hoped and aspired. Seven successive generations of them have swept out from the unknown, and into the unknown have vanished again. The ambitious statesmen, the mother not to be comforted in the loss of her child, the passionate patriot, the disso-

CHARLES FRANCIS ADAMS.
1869.
AGED 62.

lute brawler of the tavern, — those whom hardly a world would content, and those whom a crust satisfied, — have disappeared for evermore. Ah, it is pathetic, tragic, not to be understood! All that remains with us is a name, and the good they have done. The good they have done! It is the remembrance of that which brings us here to-day. We are glad to unite in praise of that. We welcome this distinguished point in our church's history to praise goodness and all sacrifices for truth. These remain, these virtues of the men and women of the past, — a priceless heritage and a ceaseless inspiration.

And all the good work wrought by them and the fair lives of them belong peculiarly to you. Your predecessors they are, — this church theirs and yours. The same names are borne by many of you that were borne by the founders of the society. Are you sensible of the significance of that? Do you realize what it is to be in the place of your fathers, and to be continuing their work? In the great migration of peoples now proceeding, when millions are travelling far to make themselves new homes, it is something to be valued to be permitted to continue where your own have occupied for generations. This church should be to you your Mecca, your Jerusalem; every part of it and its surroundings a memorial, every name a history. From pew and pulpit, from the highways leading to this temple, from "God's acre" adjoining, visionary forms should greet you, each with its separate message, pleasant, pathetic, admonitory. A place this for thoughts, a place to engage the heart's deepest affections. And for those who later have settled here there is much to move and uplift. Is not the wealth of our traditions for all, and the joy of laboring together for all, and the promise for all that "the glory of this latter house shall be greater than that of the former"? God grant that in faithfulness we bring this to pass, and make this church not merely a remembrance in the land, but a present, a living power!

GRAVESTONES OF PASTOR TOMPSON AND TEACHER FLYNT.

1639   1889

COMMEMORATIVE SERVICES.

COMPLETION OF TWO HUNDRED AND FIFTY YEARS

SINCE THE GATHERING OF THE

First Church of Christ in Quincy.

SUNDAY, SEPT. 29, 1889,

AT 2 P.M.

HISTORICAL DISCOURSES BY THE PASTOR: SEPT. 22, AT 10.30 A.M., "THE CHAPPEL OF EASE," WHEELWRIGHT'S CHURCH AT THE MOUNT; SEPT. 29, 10.30 A.M., THE ORGANIZATION OF FIRST CHURCH AND ITS SUBSEQUENT HISTORY.

ORDER OF EXERCISES.

Organ Voluntary.
Gloria from the Twelfth Mass . . . . *Mozart.*

Invocation.
The Rev. RODERICK STEBBINS, Pastor of the First Church in Milton.

Music.
"O Sing unto the Lord" . . . . *Chandler.*

Scripture Selections.
The Rev. G. HERBERT HOSMER, Pastor of the Church of the Unity in Neponset.

Music.
Hymn, by Sternhold . . . . *Northfield.*

Prayer.
The Rev. ALFRED P. PUTNAM, D.D.

Music.
Response, "Bow down thine ear" . . . . *Davenport.*

Addresses.
The Rev. DANIEL MUNRO WILSON, Pastor.
JOHN QUINCY ADAMS BRACKETT, Lieut.-Governor of Massachusetts.
The Rev. STOPFORD WENTWORTH BROOKE, Pastor of the First Church in Boston.

Music.

Sacred Song . . . . *Solo.*

Addresses.

CHARLES FRANCIS ADAMS.

The Rev. ALFRED A. ELLSWORTH, Pastor of the First Parish Congregational Church of Braintree.

JOSIAH QUINCY.

Music.

Hymn written for the 200th Anniversary, by JOHN QUINCY ADAMS.

ALAS! how swift the moments fly!
How flash the years along!
Scarce here, yet gone already by,
The burden of a song.
See childhood, youth, and manhood pass,
And age, with furrowed brow;
Time was; Time shall be, — drain the glass, —
But where in Time is *now?*

Time is the measure but of change;
No present hour is found;
The past, the future, fill the range
Of Time's unceasing round.

Where, then, is *Now?* In realms above,
With God's atoning Lamb,
In regions of eternal love,
Where sits enthroned I AM.

Then, pilgrim, let thy joys and tears
On Time no longer lean;
But henceforth all thy hopes and fears
From earth's affections wean:
To God let votive accents rise;
With truth, with virtue, live;
So all the bliss that Time denies
Eternity shall give.

Poem.

CHRISTOPHER PEARSE CRANCH.

Music.

"Oh, Praise the Lord" . . . . J. B. Marsh.

Addresses.

The Rev. CHRISTOPHER R. ELIOT, Pastor of the First Church in Dorchester.
The Rev. JAMES DE NORMANDIE, Pastor of the First Church in Roxbury.
The Rev. JOSEPH OSGOOD, Pastor of the First Church in Cohasset.

Music.

Old Hundred.

Benediction.

The Rev. EDWARD NORTON, Pastor of the Evangelical Congregational Church of Quincy.

The First Church of Christ in Braintree was Embodied Sep. 16, 1639.
Record of the Rev. John Hancock.

MINISTERS OF FIRST CHURCH.

{ WILLIAM TOMPSON, Pastor, ordained September 24, 1639; died December 10, 1666.
  HENRY FLYNT, Teacher, ordained March 17, 1640; died April 27, 1668.

MOSES FISKE, ordained September 11, 1672; died August 10, 1708.

JOSEPH MARSH, ordained May 18, 1709; died March 8, 1725–6.

JOHN HANCOCK, ordained November 2, 1726; died May 7, 1774.

LEMUEL BRIANT, ordained December 11, 1745; resigned October 22, 1753.

ANTHONY WIBIRD, ordained February 5, 1755; died June 4, 1800.

PETER WHITNEY, ordained February 5, 1800; died March 3, 1843.

WILLIAM PARSONS LUNT, ordained June 3, 1835; died March 21, 1857.

JOHN DOANE WELLS, ordained December 27, 1860; resigned May 28, 1876.

DANIEL MUNRO WILSON, installed March 24, 1880.

COMMEMORATIVE SERVICES.

THE day on which the celebration occurred was bright, and tempered with a pleasant air. Some who were present at the services in the morning remained in the church till the afternoon. These, together with a large number who arrived in an early afternoon train, were provided with refreshments in the chapel. Long before the hour appointed the church was full, and by two o'clock every part of it was occupied. An animated and beautiful scene was presented. The pulpit and its immediate surroundings were decorated with plants and flowers, a massive cross of golden-rod suspended against the wall back of the pulpit being particularly noticeable from its contrast with the dark maroon draperies which formed its background. The memorial tablets to Presidents John and John Quincy Adams were decked with laurel wreaths, while the dates "1639" and "1889," wrought in green leaves, were conspicuously displayed upon the walls.

After the "Gloria" was sung by the choir, the Rev. RODERICK STEBBINS offered the following invocation:

INVOCATION BY THE REV. R. STEBBINS.

O THOU almighty and mysterious One! Thou who art without a beginning of days or an end of years! we come to Thee; we call upon Thy name, we beseech Thy holy presence, we worship Thee in prayer and praise and spoken word. We come to Thee on a day of memory, when the century past and gone leaves our minds grateful that we have been so blest. We trust in Thee, Thou almighty giver of all good; and may we acknowledge Thee in the rejoicings and in the thanksgivings of the hour. May we acknowledge Thee to be our Father, — the Father of the generation past, and Father of the generation yet to come. Amen.

The Rev. G. H. HOSMER read a selection of very appropriate passages from the Scripture, immediately after which the choir broke forth in the noble paraphrase of the XVIIIth Psalm by Sternhold, which ends with this stanza : —

> "The Lord descended from above, and bowed the heavens high,
> And underneath His feet he cast the darkness of the sky ;
> On cherubs and on cherubins full royally he rode,
> And on the wings of all the winds came flying all abroad."

The Rev. A. P. PUTNAM, D. D., then offered the following prayer : —

PRAYER BY THE REV. A. P. PUTNAM, D. D.

O GOD, eternal and infinitely glorious One, whom the heaven of heavens cannot contain, yet who dwellest in temples which our hands have built, and in the secret recesses of every sincere and faithful soul ! help us who are here before Thee to feel Thy presence and to celebrate Thy goodness, as we thus enter into these gates with thanksgiving, and into these courts with praise, and would fain bless and magnify Thy great and holy name. Reminded as we are by this impressive anniversary how the generations come and go, and how change is written on all earthly things, we come to Thee, and find strength and comfort in the thought that Thou art from everlasting to everlasting, — the one sure rock and refuge, almighty Father and Friend of us all forever and ever. The fathers, where are they? Where, but still with Thee in whom they put their trust, and to whom they were faithful even unto death? And in Thee, in Thee, O Lord our God, we would also repose our trust, while we pray that we may receive of Thy spirit and do Thy will. Here, on this consecrated ground, where they toiled and tended this vine that grew to such goodly growth and abundant fruit, — toiled to found the beneficent institutions under which we live and thrive, — we would thank Thee for all their pious labors and examples, and for their rich bequests to the future. We thank Thee for this ancient church of their care and love, and for all the signal favors which Thou hast vouchsafed unto it in all its continued history from the first to the last. We thank Thee for the long line of earnest and devoted pastors who have here preached Thy word, and had so many souls given them as the seals of their ministry and the crown of their rejoicing. We thank Thee for that great company of godly men and saintly women who have reverently trodden these aisles and bowed themselves here in prayer, and lifted unto Thee the voice of sacred song, and communed with the Christ, and sought to be in his likeness, and so entered into their rest. We thank Thee for all those kind and excellent teachers, and active and useful workers, who have here wisely instructed and lovingly guided throng after throng of tender youth, or in manifold other ways have wrought good for this community in which they lived. We thank Thee also for the many illustrious statesmen, rulers, reformers, and philanthropists who have here had their birth or home, and who have here caught lessons of wisdom and virtue and duty which they have carried forth to larger spheres, where in our own land or abroad, in calm or storm, in darkness or in sunshine, they have dedicated their gifts and their all to the welfare of their country and of mankind. For the purity of their heart and life, for their stern integrity, which not the clamors of party or the blandishments and temptations of the world could mar or weaken, for their service of truth and justice and freedom, the cause of good government, of sound learning and morals, and Christian truth, and for all the blessed results which they achieved we thank and bless Thee, O Thou God of our life. For the memories of the precious dead we thank and bless Thee. Not unmindful, not unobservant of this scene and of these solemnities is the great cloud of witnesses by which we are now and here surrounded. They are here with us in thought and sympathy, in love, in spirit, and in fellowship. Are they not ministering spirits unto us, and shall not we also be the heirs of salvation? Grant us more and more, we beseech Thee, of their faith, their zeal, their consecration to Thy work. Pour out Thy blessing, we pray, upon this church, upon both pastor and people; and as Thou hast been with it in time past, so wilt Thou be with it in time to come, that Christian faith and love may here abound, and go forth hence to disseminate far and wide the influences that shall be for the healing of souls and of the nation. Bless, we pray Thee, our country; and as Thou hast been with her alway and hast guided her safely thus far, as by a pillar of cloud by day and a pillar of fire by night, and hast made her prosperous among the states and empires of the earth, so wilt Thou lead her still on to a more exalted destiny, whose record shall tell of other triumphs of Thy strength, whose glad day shall see other shackles broken and other slaves made free, and more and more of faith and love and light. Bless the President of the United States and all who are in authority; we pray that they may rule in equity and righteousness, may fear God and eschew iniquity, and cleave to Thy will, and serve in their day and generation as those who shall give account. Be with us, one and all, and help us that we may be good citizens, kind and helpful neighbors and friends, and faithful and true disciples and followers of Thy dear Son. Give unto us the clear vision without which Thy people perish. Give unto us that purity which those have who see God, that truth which maketh free indeed, that faith which overcometh the world, that love which is the fulfilling of the law, that love to God and love to man which are so acceptable in Thy sight. And may we have within us those sacred fires of truth and liberty that shall quicken us to every good word and work; and may we so live that when at last we shall be called hence, and others shall succeed to our places, it shall be given to us, as to those who have gone before, to see the seed that has been sown in faith, in patience and fidelity, springing up and bearing fruit unto Thy glory. Hear us and answer us, and forgive us and bless us. We ask it in the name of Jesus Christ our Lord. Amen.

ADDRESS BY THE PASTOR.

DEAR FRIENDS, — This service we are now celebrating is the culmination of our commemorative services. Already we have had delivered by the pastor of the church two discourses in full Puritan measure, and only half that might be said has been said. But what I said this morning and a week ago this morning was intended as preparation for these services, and also that I myself might be effaced in order that persons who came from abroad and others deeply interested in the church should have an opportunity to speak.

The Rev. John Hancock says that it was on the 16th day of September, 1639, that our church was embodied. Add ten days to that for change of style, and it brings the date to the 26th, which is really the anniversary of our birth as a church. It seems to me, and I say it with all deference, that Governor Winthrop was in error when he wrote that this church was gathered the 17th of the month, and that Dr. Lunt continued the error when he celebrated the two hundredth anniversary on the 29th. To be sure we also are celebrating on the 29th; but we take the day set by Dr. Lunt in order to avoid confusion, leaving it to those who come after us to select the date more in accordance with such evidence as we possess.

The testimony of the Rev. Mr. Hancock is of first importance. He had the ancient records, now lost, in his possession; he was a careful man; and he is positive our church was embodied September 16, — that is, September 26, new style. It was a temptation also to celebrate on this present day, because being Sunday so many of the laymen would find it more convenient to be here. Of course for the same reason we are deprived of the presence of many clergymen whom we should be delighted to have with us; but ministers are quite ready to be sacrificed at any time in order that the laity may have a chance to go to church. I am put here to bid all who are present a hearty welcome, — to you the friends of this church, to you once members of it and now from a distance coming to join in this glad occasion, to all who are interested in the historical associations of this church, and to all who feel that by coming here they celebrate the memory of one of the most influential and honorable societies in the Commonwealth.

It is customary at all celebrations such as we are now taking part in for the State of Massachusetts to be represented; and heretofore, at the celebrations of the First Churches that have preceded ours in age, the State has been represented, either by the governor or by the lieutenant-governor. Our Governor writes me that he is not at all able to be present on account of illness; he has sent the following letter, which I shall read: —

BOSTON, September 21, 1889.

Mr. LEWIS BASS and Rev. D. M. WILSON, Quincy, Mass.

DEAR SIRS, — I greatly regret that I shall not be able to attend the exercises on Sunday the 29th instant, in commemoration of the founding of the First Church in Quincy. In such an event I take deep interest, as its occurrence indicates the vitality of those principles which led to the settlement of, and which are influencing the development of, this country.

Your church and society have fame throughout this broad land and beyond its limits, in that two of those who have been numbered among its members have been selected to fill the highest office in the gift of our people. Both of them were giants among the men of their days. They have gone, and your church edifice is the shrine of their honored dust; but the influence of their lives remains for our instruction and benefit, and for that of coming generations of Americans.

We have with us their descendants whom we delight to honor, not so much because of their ancestry as for their worth and ability. The Adams family, the First Church in Quincy, the City of Quincy, are so closely united that they are essentially parts of one whole, centres of right influence, of energetic action, of prosperity, of sobriety in all things, — in a word, examples of New England, its civilization, its institutions, and its growth.

I am yours very respectfully,

OLIVER AMES.

Now, as the Governor could not be present, an invitation was sent to John Quincy Adams Brackett, not only because he would represent the State, but because of his name. Brackett, Adams, Quincy, — when has this church been without these names? And in every generation those who bore them honored this church and their country, were useful and admirable members of the community. Sorry I am that on account of illness, also, he is not here to represent not only the State, but the names which he bears.

You all understand, because I presume you have all read the history of the early days of the colony, that this church reaches back in its existence to the year 1636. For two or more years before First Church was organized, worshippers met here, but they did not then form an independent congregation. They went to their meeting-house in Boston, and there received the sacrament. They went ten miles from here to the city — then the town — of Boston, to attend this occasional service. The pastor at that time was John Wilson, and it is somewhat of a coincidence that Wilson is the name of the present pastor of the church which originated in the members of the Boston church who lived here. But we have with us the pastor of Boston's First Church, and he will remember that when the people here wanted to withdraw from his church and have a church of their own, his church felt so poor it feared that the number of persons going from them would weaken it, and they were loath to give their consent. But they had the shrewdness to tax the people of this place for the support of their church when they finally gave permission, and as they "grew up with the country" they eventually prospered, and, I am pleased to say, can now get on without any support from us.

I have the pleasure of introducing to you the Rev. STOPFORD WENTWORTH BROOKE, pastor of the First Church in Boston.

ADDRESS BY THE REV. S. W. BROOKE.

LADIES AND GENTLEMEN, — I must confess that when I received the kind invitation of your minister and committee, I experienced some feelings of awkwardness and incongruity at having to speak to you on such an essentially American occasion as the present. But with that hospitality, which is so delightful a characteristic of this country and for which I have had so often to be grateful, you have been good enough to forget that I am not an American citizen. You have remembered only that I am the minister of the First Church in Boston. It is as such that I bring you the warm greetings of the ancient mother church out of which you sprang, on having completed two hundred and fifty years of your corporate life. 1 had hoped indeed that another representative of that Church, one whose name is associated in your minds with occasions such as this, one whose extraordinarily intimate and varied acquaintance with the facts of New England history we all recognize and admire, — Dr. George Ellis, — would have been here to speak to you about the early relations of the two churches. It would not be wise however for me, even if I had the requisite knowledge, to trespass on his ground; and you — you who know the general outline of those facts so well yourselves — would scarcely thank me for what you might well call such English audacity. I shall say nothing, therefore, about the mutual history of the two churches; but I will rather, as a Unitarian clergyman speaking to Unitarian laymen, confine myself to two thoughts applicable to our present Unitarian position, which have been suggested by this happy occasion. They are common thoughts; but I need not therefore ask your indulgence for them, for it is common thoughts after all that most rule our lives.

The first is that the men who founded these churches were men possessing — nay, rather possessed by — a great idea. They left England, its comforts, and all the dear associations that brooded for them in those meadows and quiet villages of the eastern countries, they endured this inhospitable climate, they faced ferocious enemies, the terrors of the wilderness, and the doom of death for many of their number, because they desired to worship and serve their God according to the inmost convictions of their souls. They would not compromise with what they considered the truth, they would not conceal it out of indifference or fear or self-interest; but holding it dearer than all outward happiness, they sought a place where they might live by their truth in freedom. That is a memory which must have been in the minds of many of us to-day; it is a thought which we shall do well to cherish. We live in an age which congratulates itself on the growth of tolerance between the different sects of religion. But is there not real danger lest in this spread of the tolerant spirit we should forget, as these men never did, that there is a virtue in thinking out our own opinions, in making them part of our very life, and in standing by them in the face of the world? I meet Unitarians and liberal Christians sometimes — I do not allude to professed non-churchgoers — who seem to have no religious convictions whatever; they consider one intellectual form of faith as good as another, although they are very certain in their intellectual doctrines about business or politics; they frequent the church where their friends go or fashion and wealth lead, although views are held and ceremonies performed there with which they do not and cannot sympathize. That was not the spirit which drove these men whose memory we celebrate to-day into the primeval forest across a terrible ocean; that was not the spirit which has made these churches so strong and enduring. They were in earnest about their religious thoughts; they meant them to rule their lives; they believed they were the very truth itself; they were prepared to suffer and die for them. Better I say their earnestness with all its fearful intolerance — and it was fearful — than our sentimental tolerance without their earnestness of conviction.

There is another thought suggested by this occasion, which you will permit me to put before you. It is that the men who founded these churches intended they should be centres whence other centres of intellectual and spiritual influence should radiate through the land. In Virginia, as Mr. Lodge has recently told us, " the mass of the clergy were men who sold tobacco, were the boon companions of the planters, hunted, shot, and drank hard." With some of these occupations I have no quarrel; but the gist of his condemnation comes when he adds that they performed " their sacred duties in a perfunctory and not always decent manner." But in New England the clergy were some of the most cultivated and serious men of their time. With all their faults, — faults which belonged to their age as much as to themselves, and few of us who realize how difficult it is to be above one's age will condemn them harshly for these, — they yet represented and kept vigorous and intelligent that stern doctrine and that rigid moral tone of their society, without which it could never have conquered its extraordinary difficulties and dangers; and so highly did they prize this doctrine and this tone that in every new settlement they established a church of their faith, and secured thus the spread of their views and their spirit. Is not that too an ideal which our churches — the lineal descend-

ants of those stern and fiery men — would do well to remember?
I am well aware, when I say this, that the Unitarian churches
of New England have always represented a powerful intellectual and moral influence in the community. It would not be
becoming for me to remind you of that new spiritual awakening to which in their early days they gave birth here, to speak
of their part in the Antislavery agitation or in the great war,
or in the saving of California to the Union. You know too,
better than I do, how many are the benevolent institutions they
founded in Boston and other cities. But still, with the exception of Mr. Starr King's lonely venture by the waters of the
Pacific, — and it was as a patriot rather than a Unitarian that he
worked there, — they have confined their range as churches too
much to New England. As individuals indeed they have accomplished much elsewhere. It is a well-known fact that to-day some
of the most intrepid commercial enterprises, much of the best literature and of the more progressive politics of the country, owe
part of their vitality and success to members of our churches.
As individuals they have indeed fulfilled the ideal of those from
whom they have sprung. But where in the new settlements are
the churches those ancestors in their zeal would have established
there? Where are the centres in the States toward the sunset
whence our intellectual and spiritual influence is to radiate
through the land? Where is the corporate body more powerful
than one or two isolated individuals can ever be, which is to
cherish and spread our doctrine and spirit as those early settlers did theirs? Those centres are unfortunately few and far
from one another. We need therefore much more of their temper of zeal. There is a great deal no doubt in the methods
they employed from which we must keep ourselves free. They
were far too fond of monopoly in religion; they applied the
trust-system ruthlessly to Christianity; they considered themselves, those old English squires and yeomen, "the lords of
human kind;" "pride in their port, defiance in their eye," they
brooked no opinion, endured no morality, which was not their

own. They would have made the whole world Puritan if they could, and if God had not been different to their idea of Him. It is a fault, however, that an Englishman can scarcely condemn severely in them without condemning severely his whole nation; it is a quality too, of which I am bound to say — if you will permit me to say it — that I have found no deficiency whatever in Americans. Their bitter intolerance indeed we shall in these days of religious liberty probably avoid; it smacks too much of High Church Episcopalianism or narrow Orthodoxy to suit a Unitarian. But their aggressive zeal; their resolve to plant their doctrines and morality and spirit wherever they could find a foothold in men's minds and hearts; their surprise, not to use a stronger word, if a new settlement refused one of their churches, — of that temper we Unitarians can, for some time to come, have a great deal more without running much risk of falling like Saint Peter, or becoming like the Sons of Thunder. Like the founders of these churches, let us assume then actively that we are born to rule the earth, and do our best to establish that rule wherever we can.

Ladies and gentlemen, these are the two thoughts which this happy occasion has suggested to me. Whether the First Church would altogether approve of them I cannot say. They have given me, however, the privilege of bringing to you — it is pleasant to repeat pleasant messages — their heartiest congratulations on having attained — how shall I express it? — nearly the age of the first great Pilgrim of the Invisible, our father Abraham. And in conclusion I can only ask you, if you have found any thing to disapprove of in what I have said, to remember that I am not yet New Englandized, — or, shall I say rather, not yet Americanized.

Mr. L. H. H. JOHNSON then made a statement regarding distinguished persons who had been unable to attend the services. He said: —

It was a disappointment to those who had charge of the invitations, it will be a matter of deep regret to those of you who

Rev. William Smith.   Rev. Peter Whitney.   Hon. Richard Cranch.
William P. Lunt, D. D.   Rev. D. M. Wilson   Rev. J. D. Wells.

were privileged to worship here during his pastorate, that the Rev. JOHN D. WELLS could not be with us to-day. He is the only one living of the former pastors of this church, and it would have been peculiarly fitting and appropriate, could his voice have been heard on this occasion of her rejoicing, this anniversary of her birth. In his absence, let me read you his letter.

BOSTON, Sept. 19, 1889.

MY DEAR MR. WILSON, — Were it not that I have for some time felt myself unequal to the demands of public occasions, I should be glad to accept your kind invitation to take part in the celebration of the two hundred and fiftieth anniversary of the First Church of Quincy. The occasion is one of deep interest to all concerned in the history and the welfare of the ancient parish, and of no little moment — permit me to say — to me, whose privilege it was so recently, and for so long a season, to occupy the place which you now fill.

To all my former parishioners, and to your whole people, let me extend my hearty greeting and my congratulations that they have lived to see this day, on which I trust they will not only renew their fealty to the faith and freedom of the fathers by whom the church was founded, but will dedicate themselves afresh to the service of a far higher faith and wider freedom than the fathers ever dreamed of, — looking forward with confidence to the dawn of that distant but surely coming day, when the clouds of ignorance and superstition that still obscure the heavens shall have utterly dissolved and vanished, and the very truth of God shall shine everywhere, undimmed and unobstructed.

I am sincerely yours, JOHN D. WELLS.

Many other letters have been received by the committee, among them one from Mr. BRECK, of Milton, an old gentleman of nearly ninety-two. I am going to read a short extract from his letter, because it gives an interesting picture of the church as it appeared during service about 1811.[1] I have here, also, letters from the pastor of the First Church of Exeter, N. H., the

---

[1] For this and other letters see later pages.

church which Rev. John Wheelwright founded when driven out of this neighborhood; from President ELIOT; from Rev. Dr. STORRS, of Brooklyn, N. Y.; from Dr. OLIVER WENDELL HOLMES, whose Dorothy Q., not John Hancock's, as he is careful to say, was born just a century before him, and from many others. All the letters are most interesting, and only the fear of taking too much time from those who are to follow prevents me from reading them.

THE REV. MR. WILSON: The next speaker I shall introduce to you is one who by his knowledge of the facts of our church and town history, by his deep interest in all that has happened in New England's past, and by his appreciation of the spirit which led to the planting of our institutions, is highly qualified to speak to you on this occasion. Indeed, it would have been entirely acceptable to the committee having charge of these exercises if he had consented to consume the larger portion of the time devoted to this celebration. I am sure you will welcome in this hour Mr. CHARLES FRANCIS ADAMS.

ADDRESS BY CHARLES FRANCIS ADAMS.

IN one of the best known and most deservedly popular of his poems, Oliver Wendell Holmes has said: —

> "Little of all we value here
> Wakes on the morn of its hundredth year,
> Without both feeling and looking queer.
> In fact, there's nothing that keeps its youth,
> So far as I know, but a tree and truth."

What is true of a century is, it goes without saying, much more true of that period of time the close of which we to-day are here to commemorate. But after all, like most other true things, it is true only comparatively speaking and in part. It is true of things human; it is in nowise true of things truly divine, or of natural processes which work out results regardless of time, as mortals reckon it. We and our fathers before us have lived here in Quincy two centuries and a half, through all those years worshipping within these walls, or within the other and humbler walls which preceded these. Two centuries and a half seem to us, and measured by the record of human events they indeed are, an epoch; yet not long since, as I was one day walking here in Quincy with an eminent man of science, we stopped on the brink of a tarn in one of our abandoned quarries. The ledge chanced to be of slate, the thin strata of which stood perpendicularly to the water, which lay at their base. Pointing up, my companion called my attention to a line of fracture near the top of the wall of stone, and perhaps a foot below the thin herbage which grew from the layer of soil which overspread it. The fracture was distinct and uniform, — just such a regular even break as you might see if some great weight were to pass over the narrow end of a bundle of shingles resting upright, and crush them all at a single point in one direction. As I looked wonderingly at this break in the solid rock, — the fractured tops of the slate all inclining to the southwest, — my companion told me that it was caused by the movement of the glacier during the ice age of America. The ice age of America! He spoke of a period so remote that the mention of it reduces all records made by man to mere memoranda of things of yesterday. Yet there before me was that line of surface fracture in the rock, — clean, uniform, distinct, — just as the towering, grinding wall of ice had left it, when, its steady march to the southward coming to a close, it had, thousands of years ago, slowly and sullenly receded in the direction of those remote regions of the frozen north where it still reigns supreme. The break in the wall of slate had been there where I looked then upon it, the same in every minute particular, from that time to this; it was there when the Scripture records say that Adam and Eve dwelt in Eden; it was there when Moses led the children of Israel up out of Egypt; it was there when Greek and Persian were contending at Marathon and Thermopylæ; it was there during the twenty centuries of Roman empire; it was there when Columbus first set foot on American soil; it was there — it had been there ten thousand years — when yesterday, as it were, our fathers, a mere handful, gathered here together on that September day and founded this church.

Viewed in this light, in the light of Nature and of God, the event we commemorate seems, and is, dwarfed of its age and brought very near to us. A thousand years measured in this scale become but as yesterday, or a watch in the night; and the signing of the Braintree Church compact was something which occurred in the morning, while we here have now come to high noon. We are here but to celebrate the event of to-day's earlier hours; yet few of the human institutions which existed in those earlier hours of Nature's single day exist now. The record is almost appalling when we recall the number of the creations of man this church of Braintree, in its quiet, steady, unbroken span of life, has survived. On that 26th of September, 1639, when Governor Winthrop sailed from the town of Boston across the bay to Braintree to meet those reverend pastors, Hobart and Wilson and Mather and Allen, who had found their way hither through the forest paths to extend the right hand of fellowship to William Tompson and Henry Flynt, history, as we know it, had scarcely yet begun. Galileo, the father of modern astronomy, was still living and learning; and John Milton, a man in the flower of his youth, had just returned to London from his memorable sojourn in Italy. Scarcely a dynasty in Europe which now exists existed then. Russia was an unknown and barbarous region, not yet admitted into the number of civilized States, for a whole generation of men was to pass away before Peter the Great rocked in his cradle. Prussia was to be created; Gustavus Adolphus had died at Lutzen only seven years before; the Thirty Years' War was still raging, and Sweden was the first military power in Europe. Poland has since been obliterated from the list of nations; but Poland then was the bulwark of civilization, for it was more than forty years later that John Sobieski smote the Turk before the walls of Vienna, and released Christendom forever from fear of the Islamite. Further west Richelieu, the great cardinal-duke, was organizing modern France and planting those seeds of wind which ripened in the fulness of time into the whirlwind of just a century ago. Finally, in England the second Stuart still sat upon the throne, for the famous Long Parliament had not yet been convened; John Hampden was a country gentleman, and men had yet to hear of Oliver Cromwell.

Thus, Sunday by Sunday, as our fathers through eight generations have gathered within these walls and followed through the centuries the same forms of worship, — the church steadily and unceasingly pursuing its work of modest, quiet usefulness, — in the outer world empires and dynasties have risen, culminated, and declined; the names of men marking epochs in human progress have been heard for the first time, become familiar as household words, and then been embalmed in history. In the intervals of divine service, men and women have listened on the porch of this church to rumors of the victories of Lutheran and Catholic in the time of Wallenstein and the Swede; they there discussed the issue of King and Commons in the days of the Long Parliament; they heard of the death of King Charles on the scaffold before Whitehall, and sent up prayers for the soul of the Protector when he was buried in Westminster Abbey. Marston Moor and Naseby were names as familiar and thrilling to them as Gettysburg and Appomattox are to us. King Philip's war hung a terror over them; and the story of the death of Wolfe on the heights of Abraham was no less a cause of thankfulness, here expressed in earnest prayer, than were the tidings that Washington stood within Yorktown, or that Grant was in possession of Vicksburg. This church had passed through nearly half of its existence when its doors were closed by the first tempests of the Revolution, and its pastor read from the pulpit the freshly promulgated Declaration of Independence.

All these human events have taken place in the two centuries and a half since this church — so old and yet so young — was gathered, and it has borne witness to them; yet in the sight of Him here worshipped, and in the scale in which His events are ordered, it is a new-comer, and but of yesterday. One hundred centuries have gone since the last great process of Nature left Quincy Bay, and the hills sloping to it upon which we dwell, and the granite which here breaks through the earth's crust, as we see them now. Thus this, the first church of Braintree, is old only as things human are old; but so far as America at least is concerned, who shall deny the age of an institution, or refuse honor to it, when its life of unbroken usefulness covers more than half the years which have elapsed since the voyage of Columbus? For it and for us "the past at least is secure."

The Rev. Mr. Wilson: When the old town of Braintree grew so large and its settlers pushed so far south that it was a hardship for some of them to come of a Sunday to the old meeting-house, they began to agitate the project of building a new house in a more central location. The people in this part of the town were not in sympathy with the movement, and opposed it. But finally the people at the south, quite out of patience, built a house for themselves. Even then our ancestors here treated them as Pharaoh treated the Israelites, — they would not let them go. Much ill feeling was between the two parts of the town, and it was continued for years. I am happy to state that it is now all ended, and that I have the pleasure of introducing to you to-day the minister of that congregation which earliest swarmed from us; and I can assure him that all animosity on our part has entirely ceased. The Rev. Mr. Ellsworth of the old church in Braintree.

ADDRESS BY THE REV. A. A. ELLSWORTH.

As a representative of the First Church of Braintree I can assure the pastor of this ancient First Church, speaking for her eldest daughter, that nothing but the kindest feelings are indulged by the child for the parent. And in behalf of my people, many of whom are here, I earnestly thank the committee in charge of these exercises for including us among their guests.

The extension of fellowship toward us could not be unacknowledged, although it involved the duty of speaking, amidst so rich a repast of thought and expression appropriate to the occasion, where if ever for me silence would be golden. I am glad to know that our church colonized from this in the sixty-eighth year of your age, — a period when children are very apt to leave home for local convenience and for personal happiness, and still cherish the associations of their birthplace.

During the past few days I have been reviewing in the excellent sermon of your pastor, and in many an old volume, the record of the two hundred and fifty years which are included between the dates on the programme. It is a history full of interest at every step, and becomes dramatic to one realizing that he is following back the streams of his own existence, who discovers here and there the trace of an ancestor, and thus feels the rythm of pulsations which chord with the beatings of his own heart. It is a long, full story, and were a day given each one here to speak, it could not half be told. We may, however, by the associations of this hour revive many fading memories, kindle a flame of gratitude toward those who lived in the past, become invigorated for present duties, and thus be the mediators of all the good Puritan forces which may still go marching on.

Happy the orator or historian who at some "protracted meeting" might present to his audience the many gems of character, act, or incident easily gathered out of the details of this history. The specific is always so much more interesting than the generic. But to do it justice requires talents and time not at my command.

The last speaker, Mr. Charles Francis Adams, is one who above others has both the talents and the time. The gems are not always sought for in the exhumations of the early archives, for it is frequently a diversion, requiring not talents but only time to entertain an audience with the errors and foibles of the Puritan age. Many reviewers seem to be like house-servants, sent to the attics to bring down ancient and faded wardrobes, and to excite amusement, forgetting that ancient errors largely were like clothing, — a fashion, to change and pass away.

The history of the Puritans is most important to us, not from their accidental peculiarities, but for the great eternal principles upon which rested their religion and their liberty. The rest is mere bric-a-brac, which pleases a senseless and trifling generation.

Our fathers were men of stalwart mould. Baptized in the spirit of the Reformation, they believed in the freedom and liberty of the individual soul, and out of this came a liberality that had never been seen before, say what we may of their narrowness. Much of that which we talk of as a sentiment, they lived as a principle, and made sacrifices for, that it might exist. They collected the seeds for the tree of liberty at Worms and Geneva; fostered its growth at Scrooby, Braintree, Essex, and Amsterdam; took it up rooted, with the names attached, transported it and set it out in these very fields, that they might live piously under its shade and worship God beneath its branches, and not that it might grow May-poles to be danced around.

Our fathers were reformatory, revolutionary, schismatic; and in these qualities they displayed courage and mental force, but these had not made them historic characters worthy to be so remembered. Their virtue consisted not in destruction, not in mere negation, not in breaking up old temples and housing themselves in the fragments, building nothing better for themselves, not in eliminating superstition and tyranny, — but in a vigorous grasp and hold of fundamental truth, believed in with all their heart, and for which they would contend with all their powers. Because they were Protestants they believed not less in God, but more in God. They broke with many of the symbols of the English Church only because they believed more positively in the Divine Spirit. They gave up Christmas and Easter because their firmer faith saw Christ walking every day among the churches and standing by their side amidst wolves and Indians. They held strongly to man's depravity, but they held just as strongly to his responsibility under a moral law, and thus kept the balance of his real dignity. It is shocking to some sensibilities to know that they believed the heathen a lost man, but they were not hardened fatalists to leave him untaught without the offers of salvation. Mayhew and Eliot would blaze the forest path with their bleeding feet, if only a savage might learn of "justification by faith." They developed into republicans and threw off the yoke of British rule, but they believed in law and order, and voted themselves poor that they might have schools and churches, colleges and an intelligent and righteous legislature. Shall we merely build the tombs of the prophets and garnish the sepulchre of the righteous? Do we imagine that the spiritual inertia of their positive faith is to carry us forward through all time without any added impulse? Or will the restoration of what they threw away make up for the throwing away of what they held as all important? Will our modern agnosticism, deification of science, irresponsible fatalism, and secularism secure the Church and State against man's passions, unchecked by anything that may be called a positive religion? Is it not still and always true that man's responsibility to God is the greatest truth, and that after all our good works, conscience always recognizes the fact that there is a margin of demerit only to be balanced by some method of forgiving love, and that without a distinct faith in a peopled heaven where souls are blessed, there will be little hope of blessedness among a peopled earth? I would not that you should read life backward.

> "Alas! what once hath been shall be no more;
> The groaning earth in travail and in pain
> Brings forth its races, but does not restore;
> And the dead nations never live again."

But I would make of this past history a concave mirror, catching the rays of the present day and the concentrated good principles of the past, all to be focussed into a beacon for the future, shining into years far beyond, that liberty, intelligence, and religion may never be wanting among men.

THE REV. MR. WILSON: This church has never been without the name of Quincy. It is the only name, so far as we know, which has come down to us without a break from Wheelwright's church. Nine generations of that family have worshipped in the meeting-houses of this society. They have guided the councils of it, honored it by their fame, supported it by their liberality.[1] Vessels of our communion service bear their name, and this ancient Bible was presented by one, and at a later time rebound by another among the most honorable of the family. Very interesting and instructive are the lives of the Quincys, in spite of the difficulty of distinguishing the numerous Josiahs and Edmunds from one another. I now have the pleasure of introducing to you JOSIAH QUINCY, the sixth of that name.

---

[1] The Rev. Mr. Hancock in his sermon preached the 23d of April, 1738, on the "death of the Hon. Edmund Quincy, Esq., one of his Majesty's Council, and of the Judges of the Circuit, and agent for the Province of Massachusetts Bay at the Court of Great Britain," has the following: "And in token of his peculiar affection to this church, whereof he was a leading member for many years, he has left us an acceptable legacy in his last will and testament. He loved us, and how was his heart engaged in building us a synagogue?"

ADDRESS BY JOSIAH QUINCY.

The anniversary that we celebrate to-day reminds us no less of change than of continuity. It is as significant in suggesting the reflection that ecclesiastical organizations and theological dogmas are not exempt from mutability and decay, as it is in recalling the fact that our church of to-day is the lineal descendant of that which our fathers planted at Mount Wollaston a quarter of a millennium ago, — the same church, yet so changed in its forms of worship, in its articles of faith, that its founders would scarcely be able to recognize it; the same, yet different, even as we, who have long since separated Church and State and established religious liberty, are different from our ancestors, who charged with sedition the first minister who preached here, and banished him from their Commonwealth for theological opinions maintained in a sermon.

Yet under changing form is generally to be found, if rightly sought for, unchanging substance; out of the past speaks often a living voice for the present. The Christian Church changes; Christianity remains the same. The kernel that lies concealed within the outer envelope is the same to-day as when our fathers drew from it the spirit that supported them through the trials and hardships of their young settlement; and it was the same then as when it effected that marvellous conversion of the ancient world. The famous sermon — probably delivered here at the Mount as well as before the Church at Boston — for which John Wheelwright was sent forth into the wilderness through the deep snows of winter, seems as strangely quaint to us in its theology as in its structure and spelling; yet translated into our modern forms of thought and expression, the doctrine of this discourse, which has been well described as a bold one for any age, is still glowing with the fire which blazed through it two centuries and a half ago, and may well detain us for a few moments to-day.

To support justification by faith or grace, and to deny the sufficiency of justification by works, — to use the old theological terms, — was Wheelwright's thesis; or to state generally the real essence of his side of the Antinomian controversy, of which this sermon formed a part, he maintained that a living knowledge of spiritual truth was necessary, and that right conduct alone could not take its place. The present tendency of liberal religious thought is indeed away from this opinion, while it is even more at variance with the scientific spirit of our age. But in memory of the fearless and able minister, let us briefly look at what is essential in the doctrine he upheld.

The question is really a very simple one. Does the purpose and object of our existence lie inside the world as it appears to us, or outside of it? If the former, right conduct here is all sufficient, and Christianity has its chief value as a code of ethics; if the latter, conduct cannot be the final end, but only a means to a transcendental end. Is this temporal existence of man a real and true life, of which the life eternal is only the sequence or resultant; or is the life eternal the only true life, from which man is separated by the passing illusion of existence in the material world? If we answer the first question in the affirmative, we are substantially under the covenant of works; if the second, we are under the covenant of faith or grace preached by Wheelwright.

Neither from the point of view of the individual man nor from that of the human race as a whole can outward works be regarded as a final end. The individual enters the form of perception which we call the world through the door of birth, leads a brief existence of unsatisfied striving, and passes out again through the door of death. In no true sense can it be said that our works follow us; they remain behind as part of the common inheritance of humanity, to share the fate of humanity. Some few exceptional persons, fortunate — or perhaps rather, in a deeper view, unfortunate — in the possession of peculiar temperaments or in their special circumstances, are indeed able to regard their lives in the world of sense as satisfactory and complete, needing only to be crowned with eternity, and to see in their external works the purpose of life accomplished and existence justified. But for the great mass of mankind life needs, and has everywhere and always been given, a transcendental end. In this the greatest men of action and the deepest thinkers have agreed with unlettered peasants; thus only has the human mind been able to "justify the ways of God to man." Through this church men have for two hundred and fifty years sought diligently to find that end; here two Presidents of the United States have joined with the humblest citizens of their town in seeking for light to understand it.

Nor do we reach a different conclusion as to the sufficiency of works if we merge the individual life in that of the race. If we view the human race as one continuous organism, and if we are sanguine enough to believe in the ultimate perfectibility of a society governed by worldly motives, we cannot avoid the same difficulty which meets the individual. For the words of Carlyle are true no less of the human race taken as a whole than of its separate members: "We emerge from the Inane; haste stormfully across the astonished earth; then plunge again into the Inane." Science, which sometimes seems so hostile to the claims of religion, has established some facts of the greatest value in forcing us to the conclusion that no purpose of existence can be found inside the limits of the world. One of these facts is that the human race has had a beginning and must come to an end; that the globe which we inhabit was evolved out of chaos, and only acquired after the lapse of ages those conditions which make human life possible; that in the course of other ages those conditions will again change, and human life on earth can no longer exist; and that finally what came out of chaos will return into chaos, and

> "the great globe itself,
> Yea, all which it inherit, shall dissolve,
> And, like an insubstantial pageant faded,
> Leave not a wrack behind."

The inexorable hand of time will in the end blot out all human civilization, and of man and his works there will be left no trace. When the last page of history has been written it will be, if it have no significance outside the world, "a tale told by an idiot, full of sound and fury, signifying nothing."

These considerations, which lead some minds indeed to a shallow and unphilosophical materialism which explains nothing, properly lead the way to transcendentalism. From the irresistible logic of pessimism religion offers the only escape; but it must be a religion not of works alone, not of forms or dogmas or ethics, but a religion such as Wheelwright preached, — a religion of grace, of spiritual truth. The life of sense is illusion, — its final object, to overcome itself and pass into the life eternal. Works, which are part of the illusion, are of value to him who performs them only as they bring his immortal spiritual individuality nearer to the final point of disillusion; and he who is under the covenant of grace has already attained nearer to this point than works alone can carry him. And from that grace and spiritual insight will flow, as the whole history of mankind shows, more works and better works for the benefit of others than can come from the motives supplied by any code of ethics.

In memory of another great preacher of this church let us recall the pregnant words upon this subject which he uttered at the celebration of a half century ago. "The vital principle of Christianity consists of the vindication it so triumphantly makes of the spiritual principle in man. It is a soul-religion, not only as distinguished from forms and rites, but also and still more as distinguished from a decent exterior, from a mere prudential conformity of the life to traditions and usages. It seeks to regenerate man; and this regeneration can only be effected by penetrating as it does with its light into the mind, and with its purity into the heart, and by setting up its kingdom within. . . . The struggle always has been between faith and works; between the principle of religion in the soul, and the manifestation of it in conduct; between the living spirit of piety, and dead mechanical conformity to fixed usages and forms."

The hymn which we are about to sing to-day, as it was sung at the celebration of fifty years ago, seems to me in harmony with that conception of religion which was common alike to Wheelwright, the first preacher of our earliest settlement, and to Lunt, the gifted minister who stood in his place two hundred years later. After enjoying all of earthly greatness which his country could bestow, John Quincy Adams still placed the true end and purpose of life beyond the material world, and held himself justified rather by faith than by works. Time is indeed, in his words, "the measure but of change." Eternity is the reality, time the delusion. Time and change alike are but the forms of our human consciousness. Eternity is now, and time is merely the veil which hides it from us. Religion lifts a corner of the veil and gives us a point of view, if we will but take it, outside of time, outside of the world, outside of ourselves as human beings, — the only point of view from which the universe, otherwise so incomprehensible, can be in part at least understood. Not through time to eternity, but out of time to eternity, is the true thought. And to that *now* which is "in realms above" we can attain in this present life, as did some of our fathers who "worshipped in this mountain" of old, if we will seek out the true essence of that religion which has come down to us from them. Only as man conceives of himself not as an organism of matter, endowed for a time with a mysterious quality called life, but as an immortal spirit, passing through that form of consciousness which we call the world, but neither limited to it nor having his real home in it, does life acquire its true significance. To borrow again the words of Carlyle: "Sweep-away the illusion of time! Are we not spirits, that are shaped into a body, into an appearance, and that fade away into air and invisibility? This is no metaphor; it is a simple scientific fact. We start out of nothingness, take figure and are apparitions; round us, as round the veriest spectre, is eternity."

The religion of those who come after us may change as much in form as our religion of to-day has changed from that of our ancestors; but that our descendants will continue to have a religion, and that its essence will be the same two hundred and fifty years hence that it is to-day, and was two hundred and fifty years ago, we may rest well assured. I can close with no better wish for the future of this church of our fathers than that it may again number among its ministers some Wheelwright, with both the power and the courage to preach the spiritual truth and spare not, though his condemnation fall upon his fellow ministers and cause "combustion in church and commonwealth;" among its laymen, some Coddington, ready to abandon home and worldly possessions rather than give up his convictions; and among those from other places who here listen to the Word, some Henry Vane, ready to vindicate the great principles of civil and religious liberty even by laying down his life upon the scaffold, with the calm fortitude taught by the gospel of Christ.

The congregation was invited to rise and join in singing the hymn written for the two hundredth anniversary by John Quincy Adams. The great company present stood up and sang two verses with fervor. Then the Rev. Mr. WILSON spoke as follows: —

About fifty years ago when the town of Quincy and all the towns of old Braintree celebrated their two hundredth anniversary, the citizens were disappointed in not securing President John Quincy Adams to deliver the oration. The affair was likely to go by default, when the young men of the town came to the rescue, and without much regard to the older citizens went ahead and arranged the programme. One of the orators selected was the Rev. George Whitney, son of the venerated Parson Whitney; the young men's choice for poet was another young man, Christopher Pearse Cranch. He is our poet to-day, his youthful spirit in no degree abated, his love for this church and town as great as ever. By name and descent he is our own, he is one of us; and it is with much satisfaction I extend your welcome to him on our two hundredth and fiftieth anniversary.

POEM BY CHRISTOPHER PEARSE CRANCH.

THE mild autumnal day
Is filled with visionary forms that pass
Before our sight as in some magic glass.
    Along the horizon gray
The dim procession of ancestral shades
    Appears, dissolves, and fades.
Grave, sad-robed fathers of the Church and State,
Matrons and mothers, mild-eyed and sedate,
And sober-suited youths and home-bred maids,
    Pledged to maintain inviolate
New England's earliest, dearest heritage, —
The faith and conduct of that sterner age.

Westward across the rough and unknown seas
We see them, an advancing, spreading host, —
    Along the rocky coast
And 'neath the forests of primeval trees
Building their simple states and villages;
And in their midst, like castles of defence
In mediæval days, to guard the tents
And cottages of those who clustered round,
    Choosing a plot of ground
Whereon they found a church, though called by a name
    Of more prosaic sound
Than in the stately cities whence they came,
Where proud cathedrals with their chanting choirs

Stretch their long aisles and lift their solemn spires.
   Here first of all they rear
With pious hands and reverence austere
Their house of worship and of brotherhood,
Of prayer and praise and spiritual food,
Symbol supreme of trust and faith sincere.

Far back in shadowy lines the lives, the plans
   Of those old Puritans
Lie sketched; and though to us their acrid creeds
Seem like the harsh and unripe fruits of spring,
Fitter for ancient Hebrews than for needs
Of Saxon men who fled from priest and king
And rituals outworn, to seek across the sea
A home for conscience and for liberty,
Let us believe their virtues far outweighed
Their faults, and note their sunshine, not their shade.
True to the essence of the doctrines taught
And to the lights they saw, they lived and wrought.
Earnest and brave, in this their new abode
They found amid the wilds a surer road
Toward freedom, union, purer Church and State.
   Nothing effeminate
Or base was here. No rank malarial dews
Of courts corrupt unnerved their sturdy thews;
But like the keen salt breeze that swept along
   Their shores o'er rocks and sands,
From unknown springs a spirit hale and strong
   Inspired their hearts and hands.

Let not our wise noon-lighted century scorn
The narrow opening of their clouded morn.
The intolerance that allowed no light to shine
Beside their own in their crypt-guarded shrine,
Shut in and kept for future times a law

Of life and duty grander than they saw.
Our fathers sowed with stern humility,
But knew not what the harvest was to be.
More light, they said, would issue from God's book,
Not knowing 't was the deeper, wiser look
The soul took of itself that gave them eyes to see.
From the rough gnarlèd root they planted here,
Through storm and sun, through patient hope and fear,
There grew a fair and over-spreading tree,
With roots fast grappling in the granite rocks,
Unharmed by cold or drought or tempest shocks;
Fed by the sun and winds and seasons' change,
It reared its trunk serenely tall and fair,
Its boughs diverging in the upper air
   Of thought and liberty,
Loaded with leaves and blossoms rich and strange,
And promise of a fruitage yet to be
   In the long centuries of futurity.

The slow-paced years and ages have moved on,
Through life and death and change, through peace and war
The vast historic eras come and gone;
   And from the climes afar
Primeval woods and savage-haunted coasts
   Filled with the gathering hosts,
Till strengthening, widening, great, united, free,
Stretches the mighty continent from sea to sea.

And with increase and change what marvels rise
   Before our wondering eyes!
What new-found powers, what labyrinthine clews,
What heights, what depths, what vast encircling views! —
Religion, science, art, mechanic skill,
The enterprise of trade by seas and lands,
The teeming farm, the factory's whirling mill;
Steam like a giant with a hundred hands;

The all-recording press
Brightening the dumb world's dreary loneliness.
The voice and tone of distant friends brought near;
Sounds packed away for unborn ears to hear;
The lightning tamed, its blazing pinions furled,
   Talking around a world
By science, law, humanity subdued
   To peaceful brotherhood;
Or linked to bands and armatures of steel
Compelled to tasks of lever and of wheel,
Or caged in moony globes with dazzling ray
   Turning the night to day.
No chemic power, unchallenged, undecoyed,
No blind telluric force left unemployed;
All matter subject to the imperial mind,
Prompt to the advantage of all human kind;
The mystic stars themselves reveal to man
   In prismic hues defined
Their secret essence and their primal plan.
All Nature stoops and serves. The very sun
We apprentice as a painter. Earth and heaven are won
To run the errands of man's shrewdest thought.
In this vast net the universe is caught;
While in a larger air his spirit tends
   Toward diviner ends,
Dissolving old beliefs, affirming new,
Leaving the false behind to grasp the true;
Or ranging through the sister realm of art
   Far from the crowded mart,
Pursuing forms of beauty and of power,
Like bees from flower to flower.
And e'en Theology, resisting long
The light, shut in her fortress grim and strong,
   Endures at last the change,
And through all sects assumes a loftier range,

Untangling with wise skill the threads perplexed
Of fundamental truth and Bible text,
Dividing the pure essence from the old
Imprisoning form, the earth-dross from the gold,
The frigid product from the warm intent,
The transitory from the permanent;
No more mid strife of Antinomian wars,
Fearing the fading of its guiding stars.
From miracles and legends quaint unbound,
No mud of Genesis can clog the feet
Of those who tread the undisputed ground
Of natural law, eternal and complete,
And between science and religion see
   No conflict, but perpetual amity.

Thus freed from close-walled alleys of the past
For broad highways toward vistas grand and vast,
For us the gates of knowledge open wide,
And the soul's shining leaders side by side
Lead onward far beyond the clouded zone
Of dogmas long outgrown.
A broader faith has risen above the rim
Of the horizon, sad, perplexed, and dim,
   Wherein our fathers saw
The limits of religion, truth, and law.
The frowning visage of a creed austere,
The visions born of superstitious fear,
The paralyzing touch that laid its ban
On the free instincts of the natural man,
The curse that like a shadow followed him
   With sure relentless pace,
The imagined sins, detectives vague and grim,
The dark satanic mask upon the face
Of an all-loving Father, fade away
   In a serener day.

No stern, inevitable doom forbids
The guests of heaven and earth to share their feast;
No sad-eyed morning opes its heavy lids.
The kindling day is all one boundless east
   For us, if only true
To the great lights that broaden on our view.

But let us not forget how firm and fast
The present is still rooted in the past;
Nor, while rejoicing in our ampler space,
The slow steep steps behind us fail to trace, —
To note how gradual is the growth of truth,
How old experience dates its forms from youth.
So, looking back to those who built the shrine,
And met to hear half truths they deemed divine,
We know our fathers planted here the root
Of which the sons possess the flower and fruit.
And fitting 't is we celebrate to-day
With music, wise discourse, and poet's lay,
   And floral offerings gay,
The first small gathering of one little band,
The simple house in a wild alien land,
Whose spiritual corner-stone we trust
Still stands, although its founders sleep in dust.

These walls, why are they reared?
Not only for old memories long endeared,
   Nor to perpetuate
Sacred traditions of an olden date;
But for truth loosed from tyrannizing creeds,
And proved in doctrines less than in the deeds;
For weekly interludes of thought and prayer,
Seclusions of release from work and care,
Serene transitions from the world of sense
To the heart's inmost fortress of defence;

LIBERTATEM AMICITIAM FIDEM RETINEBIS

D. O. M.

Beneath these Walls
Are deposited the Mortal Remains of
JOHN ADAMS,
Son of John and Susanna (Boylston) Adams,
Second President of the United States.
Born 8 October 1735.
On the fourth of July 1776
He pledged his Life, Fortune and Sacred Honour
To the INDEPENDENCE OF HIS COUNTRY.
On the third of September 1783
He affixed his Seal to the definitive Treaty with Great Britain
Which acknowledged that Independence,
And consummated the Redemption of his Pledge.
On the fourth of July 1826
He was summoned
To the Independence of Immortality,
And to the JUDGMENT OF HIS GOD.
This House will bear witness to his Piety;
This Town, his Birth-Place, to his Munificence;
History to his Patriotism;
Posterity to the Depth and Compass of his Mind.

At his Side
Sleeps till the Trump shall sound
ABIGAIL,
His beloved and only Wife,
Daughter of William and Elisabeth (Quincy) Smith.
In every Relation of Life a Pattern
Of Filial, Conjugal, Maternal and Social Virtue.
Born November 11 1744.
Deceased 28 October 1818.
Aged 74.

Married 25 October 1764,
During an Union of more than Half a Century
They survived in Harmony of Sentiment, Principle and Affection
The Tempests of Civil Commotion;
Meeting undaunted, and surmounting
The Terrors and Trials of that Revolution
Which secured the Freedom of their Country;
Improved the Condition of their Times;
And brightened the Prospects of Futurity
To the Race of Man upon Earth.

PILGRIM,

From lives thus spent thy earthly Duties learn;
From Fancy's dreams to active Virtue turn:
Let Freedom, Friendship, Faith, thy Soul engage,
And serve like them thy Country and thy Age.

For upright lives, for strength and love and grace;
For service of our country and our race;
For symbols of the unseen world that lies
About and in us, loftier than the skies,
Deeper than earth and sea, amid the war
Of worldly aims the soul's unchanging star
    Of safety in the stress
And tide of passion and of selfishness.

And gladly would we note the noble lives,
The names whose memory in this place survives
In golden gleams along the historic thread
That binds the living to the immortal dead:
Those who through stormy days of battles grim
The struggling nation's counsels wisely led;
And when her pathway grew perplexed and dim,
And help was far, and hope seemed almost fled,
    Lifted her drooping head.
Those who as rulers and ambassadors maintained
The strength, the truth, the honor we had gained,
And through successive generations made
One name illustrious, which shall never fade;
Joined with another of an old renown, —
The name that blends with Harvard's classic shade,
And syllables your old familiar town.

Nor less should we forget the worthy sons
And daughters who through centuries lived and died
Unknown to fame. The muse of history shuns
Their hidden records; gathered side by side
In yonder burial-ground, they leave no signs
    Save in the half-obliterated lines
That tell their birth, their death. Yet not in vain,
Fathers and mothers, were your humble lives;
Each in its turn an influence that survives,

A light that shines again
In sacred memories, and in hearths and homes,
Vital as greater names that gild historic tomes.

And here permit, if memory recalls
How fifty years ago within these walls, —
   Ah, crude and callow time! —
The voice you hear intoned a youthful rhyme
To celebrate the founding of this town,
Then wearing its well-earned two-centuried crown.
Ah, fleeting years of youth! Ah, passage strange
Of scenes since then; mysterious change on change!
The venerated forms that linked my life
With ancestors revered; the joy, the strife,
The blithe companionship of younger days,
The opening vistas and the untried ways
All fade in broken visions of the past;
Yet in the mould of later years recast
They take a shape that old experience lends.
Life is not loss, but gain and growth to ends
Youth could not know, and never could foresee.
And for such faith what shrine more fit than this,
Where past and present meet as with a kiss, —
This temple consecrated in the fires
Of toil and thought through a long line of sires;
Here where the old beliefs bloom out in free
Full blossom in the soul's calm liberty,
And thoughts unknown to ancient Church or State
Through daily life now throb and penetrate.

Here may the newer faith accept and hold
All sound and reverent virtue of the old;
No lamps of vital worship left untrimmed,
   No high ideal dimmed;
No genuine buddings of a noble life

Hurt by the honest thinker's pruning knife,
While thought and feeling with united aim
Kindle and keep alive the sacred flame.

Be such the mission of the church, to link
Young hearts that feel with older minds that think, —
Reason and faith fast wedded, bound yet free,
Divinely human life their progeny.

Here may the vital truth that supersedes
   The dead forgotten creeds
Warm and persuade the hearts of young and old,
And prompt to lofty thoughts and noble deeds:
A living church, — a Christian brotherhood
In all high effort for the public good.
So may this temple gather in its fold,
Conspiring with all agencies that mould
The race to higher life, till it shall stand
   A beacon in the land,
And in the coming centuries ever shine
Steadfast, undimmed, still lit by truth divine.

The Rev. Mr. Wilson: I introduce to you now the pastor of one of the oldest churches in New England; a church with which this church has been always closely connected, — the Rev. C. R. Eliot of the First Church, Dorchester.

ADDRESS BY THE REV. C. R. ELIOT.

I bring you greetings from the old church which has stood upon Meeting-House Hill — the present structure and its predecessors — since 1670. I bring them to you from the church which has walked along the years side by side with yours, and which nine years before your church was formed had its beginning.

I come to bring these greetings from a people who have toward you, as always, feelings of friendship and sympathy. To bring you these greetings is a pleasant duty to me, the minister of the First Church. Fortunately it requires very few words to say some of the very best things; and so I can say it to you in the few words necessary, that we, the people of the First Church in Dorchester, greet you of Quincy, and assure you of our friendship and Christian love.

Thoughts come crowding upon me which, if time permitted, it might be well to speak. Perhaps you will permit me to say one or two things. Not very long ago there came into a home not a thousand miles from where I live a very old cradle, built of the strongest oak, for a very new comer out of the spirit land. I have had the privilege of looking often upon that bit of household furniture, and I have thought that if its oaken panels could speak to us, what stories they could tell! They could tell of a home far across the waters, long, long ago; they could tell of a little gathering at Plymouth, England, where a few earnest men and women came together to listen to words of their pastor, John White, and to be sent across the water to form the colony here, near to you, in Dorchester. They could tell of that long voyage from March until June, when upon the great cradle of the deep they were rocked through days and weeks and months, until to these shores they came at last in safety, and the good ship "Mary and John" cast anchor near Nantasket. These oaken panels of the old cradle could tell of many things besides. They could tell us, perhaps, some of the things which to-day have not yet been spoken here, — they could tell us of the early settlers of this land in which we live. We honor the great men whose names have come down on the pages of history, — men who have done great and conspicuous work in this country. This old cradle could tell us of the tenderness of mothers' love, of the faithfulness of many a sister in this land, of noble women to whom has been due much of the honor, much of the strength, much of the sincerity, earnestness, and nobility of the men who were able to lay the foundations of this commonwealth, of this nation, and of our church. It is to honor them, the women of those early days, that I speak.

I hold in my hand a letter, in fac-simile, of one of your statesmen whose name has been spoken here to-day, — John Quincy Adams. One sentence from that may be a part of the greeting from the old church in Dorchester. It was written in 1838: "I live in the faith and hope of the progressive advancement of Christian liberty, and expect to abide by the same in death." It may be our word to you, and yours may be the same to us, — an exhortation that we all, wherever we worship, wherever we live, may worship and live in the faith and hope of the progressive advancement of Christian liberty, and abide by the same in death. "A thousand years in Thy sight are but as yesterday when it is past, or as a watch in the night." The roots of American liberty had not their place one hundred years, or two hundred and fifty years ago, or five hundred or one thousand years ago, but far back of that. Ages have passed, and slowly the work of God has been done. God has brought the blind by a way they knew not, and has led them and is leading them in paths they have not known. Jesus little dreamed of the future progress and the wondrous history of Christianity. The American revolution found its birth only after those who first spoke here noble words for liberty had passed away. The war for the preservation of our Union was not entered upon to bring freedom to the slave, yet by paths unknown and to ends unsought has the nation been led. "I am found of them that ask not for me; I am known of them that sought me not." So was it when the Puritans came to our shores; they were not believers in liberty, but they opened the way unconsciously for us; "they builded better than they knew."

The Rev. Mr. Wilson: In the record book of the old First Church of Roxbury there is a long obituary poem upon the death of the wife of our first minister, William Tompson; other entries show the close connection of the two churches. I am going to ask you to listen for a few moments to the present minister of that church, the Rev. JAMES DE NORMANDIE.

ADDRESS BY REV. JAMES DE NORMANDIE.

It is late to ask this interested but weary parish to listen to what it was my intention to say. But I will detain you only for a moment. It may be a matter of passing regret that the First Church of Christ in Roxbury and the First Church of Christ in Quincy should have begun their history by a difference which amounted almost to a persecution; and especially that the apostle Eliot, by far the most commanding figure in the ecclesiastical history of New England, — so gentle, so sweet, so devoted, who for the trouble that it would cost him to untie his handkerchief, could fling his whole quarter's salary to one asking him for charity; who with bleeding feet wandered day after day through those woods to preach the gospel to the Indians, — that the apostle Eliot should have been willing to persecute his Brother Wheelwright in this church. But if that is a matter of passing regret, it is something at which to rejoice that such a thing could not happen to-day; and that these churches are now, as they have been so long, and as we trust they may be for centuries to come, bound together by that spirit of liberal Christianity which for years they have so bravely maintained. The apostle Eliot, as I have said, was a commanding figure in New England history. When Dean Stanley came to this country a few years ago, and was asked what places he wanted to see in America, he replied, "Two: the church where the apostle Eliot preached, and Plymouth Rock." I cannot but believe, in looking through the records of his life, that the apostle Eliot was a little unwilling to do what he did do at that time. We have however to remember that he and his colleague were Puritans of the Puritans; and we know that no sincere, devoted Puritan really meant that there should be any liberty of conscience, that anybody should worship outside the doctrines which they so bravely defended, in which they lived, and for which they were willing to die. The early records of these churches are much the same in their nature, and a review of them for the past two centuries might be made very helpful as well as most interesting to this congregation, as you, sir, have shown. They tell us, these records, of a race of men who were willing to sacrifice everything for the spiritual realities in which they believed, — of a race of men that knew no sacrifice too great, who stopped at no stress of weather, and no weariness of week-day work, to gather into the sanctuary. Why, we find mention in these early records of persons coming six, eight, ten, and even twelve miles, walking to church on Sunday, and carrying all the way their little children unable to walk. And then nothing would keep them back, — no little difference of opinion among themselves, no little dissension with the minister even, would keep them back from the altar of worship. It is told in the early history of the church of Bedford in this State that one Saturday afternoon the minister was heard to have a pretty sharp contention about some fences and cattle with one of his parishioners; and the contention was heard by some of the worshippers, and one of them remarked that he ventured to say that that neighbor of the minister would not be found in the church any more. But the next Sunday morning he was in his pew as usual; and after the services, one who had heard the sharp quarrel of the day before said to him, "We thought we should never see you in church after those fierce words." "I'd have you know," was the reply, "that though I did have a quarrel with my pastor, I did not have a quarrel with the gospel." What strikes us most of all in looking over these records is the earnest observance of the Sabbath which ran all through that history. There is the early record of a law of Massachusetts Colony that "for the better observance of Sunday it is hereby ordered that on Saturday afternoon, at three of the clock, all those who inhabit the plantation shall surcease from their various employments and gather for catechizing, as the minister may direct." These early records are not only interesting, they might be made exceedingly helpful; and while we pay our tribute to the early fathers of our churches, what remains for us is to consecrate ourselves to the spiritual realities for which they lived. What is it to us if we join in these historical memories, and yet forget the work for which they lived and in which they died?

THE REV. MR. WILSON: I have great pleasure in introducing the Rev. JOSEPH OSGOOD, pastor of the First Church in Cohasset, — the oldest settled minister of our denomination in this vicinity, the dear friend of Dr. Lunt and of Mr. Wells.

ADDRESS BY REV. JOSEPH OSGOOD.

THE experience of Cohasset has been almost precisely the same as the experience of Quincy or Braintree church with regard to the First Church in Boston. It was only after long years and earnest trouble that the General Court ordered the formation of the Cohasset church. This Cohasset church has always been a neighbor church. The remembrance of Peter Whitney was very frequently recalled in the Cohasset church. My immediate predecessor, Mr. Harrison Gray Otis Fitz, was brought up under Peter Whitney and Mr. Lunt. He died after a short ministry; he was a man of pure heart, earnest spirit, and one very much beloved by the congregation. I remember with great interest my long connection with Mr. Lunt. I was associated with him in various ways, and also with Mr. Wells, who was one of my most intimate friends and associates in the ministry.

But I come before you also as a descendant of the first minister of Braintree, William Tompson. My mother was christened Elizabeth Tompson in memory of this connection; and I have been reminded by his early experiences and mission of what seems to me to have been a kind of mission of the Quincy church. You who have looked into the history will remember that he was sent as a missionary to Virginia. After a voyage of three months he arrived on the shores of Virginia. His labors did not seem to have been very successful there, though he brought back one convert, who was highly prized in the early Puritan church. The Virginians were rather glad to get rid of him, and did not wish to have their peculiar religious institutions interfered with. This was one of the earliest missionary operations in the country, and it is significant as indicating in a certain sense the spirit of the Quincy church. Years passed by, and another of your citizens was sent; and it was his high privilege to nominate as the commander of the armies of the Revolution a Virginian,—thus returning good for evil, and performing in a certain way, in a true spirit, that kind of mission which Mr. Tompson was sent to perform in the early history of the church. Has it not been one of the great privileges of this church to send forth throughout the country words of religious and spiritual freedom, words of pure patriotism, words of high statesmanship; and has not this church been carrying out the very work which in the ministry of the First Church was inaugurated? I remember talking with Charles Francis Adams the elder, just as he was about to start for his important mission as a member of Congress, about the future of political parties, and about the organizing of the House of which he was a member,— the House which was organized only after a long struggle. Have you ever thought what effect has been produced by these men speaking for civil liberty, for pure statesmanship, and exerting themselves as they have done for the progress, freedom, and prosperity of the country? As these services are about to close, can I say any better word to you for your future than to take example from the past, and as your fathers have been, so try to be yourselves in the future, carrying the highest principles of spiritual, religious, and civil freedom and uprightness and national honor into all the States of the Union, and not only into the States of the Union, but also into all parts of the world? For our civilization and our culture are such that a true word in behalf of religion, in behalf of freedom, in behalf of patriotism, in behalf of the highest interests of man, is flashed over the whole civilized world, and may be like good seed sown in good ground, producing a hundredfold to the glory of God.

The entire congregation joined in singing "Old Hundred," and the services were closed with the benediction pronounced by the Rev. C. R. Eliot in the absence of the Rev. Edward Norton.

During the exercises the pastor asked all those to stand who had been present fifty years before at the two hundredth anniversary. It was ascertained that the following persons participated in the celebration of both anniversaries: —

Miss Nancy Brackett,	Relief B. Floyd,
Samuel E. Brackett,	Wm. L. Brackett,
Miss E. C. Adams,	Mrs. Wm. L. Brackett,
Mrs. Sarah C. Underwood,	Mrs. Amos Warren Stetson,
Mrs. Ebenezer Adams,	Susanna B. Marsh,
Edwin W. Marsh,	Geo. L. Gill,
J. Franklin Burrell,	Mrs. Geo. L. Gill,
Mrs. Jos. F. French,	Edwin Gill,
Dexter Pierce,	Franklin Curtis,
Christopher P. Cranch,	Mrs. M. A. Perkins,
Mrs. Ann E. Baxter,	Mrs. Chas. A. Spear,
Susanna G. Field,	Mrs. Adams Whitney,
Lucy A. Floyd,	Miss Ann Curtis.

1639. — 1889.

The First Church — Quincy.

Cordially invites

to attend the services commemorating of its completion of

Two Hundred and Fifty Years.

Sunday, September 29th at 2 o'clock, P. M.

Charles Fitcham,
Lewis Bass, } Committee
Edward W. Gavson, } on
William F. Warren. } Invitations.

LETTERS OF CONGRATULATION.

A VERY large number of congratulatory letters were received by the Committee on Invitations. Most of these are interesting, some of them remarkably so; and to leave any unpublished bears a look almost of a lack of due appreciation. But in order to bring these pages within the designed limits a selection had to be made. So, for the most part, there are here preserved letters illustrating historical facts, or from persons connected in an especial way with the Quincy Church and Quincy people.

LETTER FROM WHEELWRIGHT'S EXETER CHURCH.

EXETER, N. H., Sept. 18, 1889.

MR. LEWIS BASS.

DEAR SIR, — I thank you most heartily for the invitation to the two hundred and fiftieth anniversary of the church which Rev. John Wheelwright ministered to, as first pastor, at Mount Wollaston, now Quincy. It would give me much pleasure to be present, if possible, — to look upon the faces of some of the men who have inherited from Wheelwright his sturdy independence of character and resistance to tyranny, whether royal or ecclesiastical, and for a few hours to breathe with you the very atmosphere of freedom.

The New England of to-day is under immense obligation to Wheelwright and to other heretics of like indomitable spirit, as well as to your famous Adams family, for the privilege of thinking and speaking its deepest and truest convictions as to whatever concerns the welfare of man.

Twice at least the Christian Church has held full sway. Once in Europe in the Middle Ages, under the Catholic supremacy; and again in Massachusetts, under the Puritan supremacy. To what were its failures due? I think, in the latter case, Mr. Brooks Adams, speaking in the mildest terms, would say, to the misinterpretation of the spirit of the Founder of Christianity.

But enough of this. I do not quite see why you celebrate your anniversary in 1889. Why not 1886? Unless I am in error in the matter, according to "Winthrop's Journal" and the "Short Story," several of the Boston communion, who had desired Wheelwright's settlement over the Boston church in conjunction with Wilson and Cotton (which settlement Winthrop resisted and prevented), were desirous to form a church at Mount Wollaston, where they resided and cultivated farms; and it was voted without objection, upon their application, that Wheelwright be assigned to them as their preacher. He at once, in October 1636, at the age of forty-four, commenced his pastoral labors at that place, — afterwards called Braintree, now Quincy. So far as appears, Wheelwright discharged his duties faithfully and acceptably at Mount Wollaston, until he was banished from Massachusetts in November, 1637. In April, 1638, he was negotiating with the Indians for a tract of land in and around what is now Exeter, where he established in that year the First Church. But perhaps you have some most valid reason for the present date of celebration.

Our own celebration in June, 1888, of the two hundred and fiftieth anniversary of the town and church was full of interest to all our people, and an occasion long to be remembered.

I sincerely hope your own celebration will be worthy of the occasion and of the distinguished men who have added lustre not only to your town and State, but to our country.

Very respectfully,   SWIFT BYINGTON.
(*Pastor First Church, Exeter.*)

FROM THE REV. A. C. NICKERSON, OF EXETER.

EXETER, N. H., Sept. 23, 1889.

To Messrs. CHARLES F. ADAMS, LEWIS BASS, EDWARD H. DEWSON, AND WILLIAM L. FAXON, COMMITTEE.

GENTLEMEN, — From a New England town which a year ago celebrated its quarter millennial I send you greeting on the occasion of the two hundred and fiftieth anniversary of the first parish of Quincy, Mass. Your first minister, the Rev. John Wheelwright, a graduate of Sidney College, Cambridge, England, was also the first pastor here, and the founder of our town. The same religious freedom which here he sought it has been the province and the pleasure of your church to maintain, and as your altars, sanctified by the dust of two of America's strongest and freest sons, shall resound with fervent praises, we tender to you and your parish our earnest felicitations.

Very respectfully yours,

A. C. NICKERSON.

(*Pastor of the Unitarian Church, Exeter, N. H.*)

FROM THE REV. EDWARD E. HALE, D.D.

ROXBURY, MASS., Sept. 17, 1889.

MY DEAR WILSON, — I am very sorry to say that I cannot be here on the 29th. I have an engagement of some time standing which I cannot change.

You have my best congratulations on so remarkable an anniversary, and my best hopes that for a quarter of a millennium more the church may be as useful and as prosperous.

Always truly yours,

EDW. E. HALE.

OLIVER WENDELL HOLMES AND "DOROTHY Q."

BEVERLY FARMS, MASS., Sept. 18, 1889.

MY DEAR SIR, — I regret that I shall not be able to have the pleasure of being present at the services on the 29th of September. I feel as if the shade of my great-grandmother, Dorothy Quincy, would be there, with those of many others whose lineage I share by my maternal ancestry.

I was pleased to learn from your note that " Dorothy Q." — *my* Dorothy, not Governor Hancock's, who was her niece — was born in 1709, — just a hundred years before I came into atmospheric existence.

I trust we shall have a full account of the commemoration, and shall look forward to it with much interest.

               Believe me, dear sir,
                  Very truly yours,
                     OLIVER WENDELL HOLMES.

FROM THE REV. R. S. STORRS, D.D.

SUNSET RIDGE, SHELTER ISLAND HEIGHTS,
Sept. 18, 1889.

Messrs. CHARLES F. ADAMS, LEWIS BASS, EDWARD H. DEWSON, WILLIAM L. FAXON, Committee.

GENTLEMEN, — I should be most happy to accept the invitation with which you have honored me, and to attend the services in commemoration of the completion of two hundred and fifty years in the history of the first church within the ancient limits of Braintree; but public duties require my presence elsewhere on the day of your proposed celebration.

Your stone temple, built in my boyhood, used to excite my admiring awe whenever I passed it in my father's chaise or in Mr. Gillett's stage-coach. I thought it then probably a rival of

DOROTHY Q.

[From the Original Painting.]

DOROTHY Q.

GRANDMOTHER'S mother: her age, I guess,
Thirteen summers, or something less;
Girlish bust, but womanly air;
Smooth, square forehead with uprolled hair,
Lips that lover has never kissed;
Taper fingers and slender wrist;
Hanging sleeves of stiff brocade, —
So they painted the little maid.

On her hand a parrot green
Sits unmoving and broods serene.
Hold up the canvas full in view, —
Look! there's a rent the light shines through,
Dark with a century's fringe of dust:
That was a Red-Coat's rapier-thrust!
Such is the tale the lady old —
Dorothy's daughter's daughter — told.

Who the painter was none may tell,
One whose best was not over well;
Hard and dry, it must be confessed,
Flat as a rose that has long been pressed;
Yet in her cheek the hues are bright,
Dainty colors of red and white,
And in her slender shape are seen
Hint and promise of stately mien.

Look not on her with eyes of scorn, —
Dorothy Q. was a lady born!
Ay, since the galloping Normans came,
England's annals have known her name!
And still to the three-hilled rebel town
Dear is that ancient name's renown;
For many a civic wreath they won,
The youthful sire and the gray-haired son.

Oliver Wendell Holmes.

BORN IN THE OLD QUINCY MANSION.

Dorathy, ye Daughter of Edmund Quinsey, Esqr., & M^s Dorathy, his wife, was born ye 4th January, 1709. — *Braintree Records.*

BAPTIZED BY THE REV. JOSEPH MARSH.

Colonel Quincey's family all baptized, April 30, 1721. — *First Church Records.*

ADMITTED TO FULL COMMUNION BY THE REV. JOHN HANCOCK.

Dorothy, daughter of Col. Quincy, May 28, 1727. — *First Church Records.*

MARRIED to Edward Jackson, of Boston, December 7, 1738.

DIED in 1762.

Her son, Jonathan Jackson, had a daughter Sarah, who married the Rev. Abiel Holmes, father of Oliver Wendell Holmes.

Solomon's Temple at Jerusalem, with Rev. Mr. Whitney for its high priest. This early impression might not be altogether reproduced if I were to be with you now; but I hope that a Christian prosperity and usefulness, solid and spacious, may mark the progress of your Society through its second quarter-millennium.

Very truly yours,   R. S. STORRS.

FROM THE REV. THOMAS HILL, D.D.

PORTLAND, ME., Sept. 23, 1889.

To CHARLES F. ADAMS, LEWIS BASS, and others. Committee.

BRETHREN IN CHRIST, — I am sorry that it will not be in my power to join with you in the celebration to which you so kindly invite me for next Sunday afternoon. My interest in the First Church, Quincy, goes back nearly, if not quite, to the time when my first interest in national politics made me grieve that one of its most honored members failed of re-election to the Presidency of the United States; and that interest has by no means been diminished by the very pleasant recollections which I carry now for nineteen years of the kind way in which many attempts to serve you were received during the temporary absence of your pastor.

Very truly yours,   THOMAS HILL.

FROM THE REV. CALEB D. BRADLEE, D.D., PH.D.

BOSTON, Sept. 17, 1889.

LEWIS BASS, Esq., Quincy, Mass.

DEAR SIR, — I have received this day your very kind invitation, in behalf of the committee, to attend the services in commemoration of the two hundred and fiftieth anniversary of the foundation of the First Church, Quincy, that are to take place on Sunday, September 29, at 2 P.M.; and although my engagements on the day named will be such as not to permit me to be present, none the less do I thank you, and those whom you represent, for the courtesy extended, and rejoice with you in your sacred memories of the past, in your great success in the present under the consecrated teachings of your faithful pastor, and in your glorious hopes for the future.

Respectfully,

CALEB D. BRADLEE.

FROM MR. CHARLES BRECK, AGED NINETY-TWO.

To LEWIS BASS, Esq. For the Committee of Invitation for the Celebration of the Two Hundred and Fiftieth Anniversary of the First Church in Quincy.

GENTLEMEN, — For your kindness in remembering me you have my sincere thanks. Under other circumstances I should have been most happy to have joined you in celebrating the day; but the weight of almost fourscore and twelve years admonishes me to be very careful about exposing myself in such public meetings. There are probably but very few beside myself who can remember attending the old church longer than I can. It is seventy-eight years ago last spring since I first attended worship in that church. I remember its situation and many of its occupants very well, — the venerable and never-to-be-forgotten Rev. Peter Whitney in the pulpit, beside him the venerable James Brackett, with his ear-trumpet, that no sound or word should be lost. The deacons' seats below were occupied by Deacons Veasie and I think Spear; in the pews the venerable John Adams, Ex-President of the United States; and oft beside him in later years his honorable son, J. Q. Adams, who was one of the most attentive listeners to the discourses that I ever noticed; the Hon. Josiah Quincy, and many other distinguished characters, with their families. In the choir there was Hezekiah Bass with his large bass-viol, John Pray with his fiddle,

Capt. Josiah Bass with his noble voice to lead the singing, old Mr. Hayden, tything-man, with his long pole to keep us boys in order, and with which the disorderly were very sure to receive a smart rap.

And when I compare those times with the present, I could but wish that I was able to attend your celebration and hear something of its origin and growth to the time which I remember. There is one thing which I often think of when I compare the old churches — with their bare wooden seats, when the women were obliged to carry foot-stoves filled with coals to keep from freezing, and the men and boys sat shivering through a long service, with the thermometer near or quite at zero — with the costly churches of the present day, warmed to summer heat throughout, their neat and comfortable seats, and short services: does pure religion keep pace with the other improvements? If so, all may be well. But when in the silent watches of the night I am conning over these things, and taking myself for an example, I think there is great room for improvement before I can hear those joyful words, "Well done, good and faithful." These things are worth pondering upon and remembering by the young as well as by the old.

In that old church I heard the first temperance discourse which I can remember, some seventy or more years ago. The Rev. Mr. Norton, of Weymouth I think, had exchanged with the Rev. Mr. Whitney. In his discourse he gave the number of inhabitants of a certain town, without naming it (some supposed it was Quincy, and that it was a plan to administer a rebuke which Mr. Whitney did not wish to do himself), and the large quantity of liquors which were consumed there yearly, and the misery which was occasioned thereby. Rum-drinking was so common in those days that the discourse made but little impression, except to be ridiculed; yet we trust that in after years his good advice, by one, at least, was not forgotten, and we trust never will be.

CHARLES BRECK.

MILTON, Sept. 22, 1889.

FROM THE REV. HENRY A. MILES, D.D.

HINGHAM, Sept. 18, 1889.

To Mr. LEWIS BASS, of the Committee of the First Church in Quincy.

DEAR SIR, — I am honored by the invitation to attend the services commemorative of the two hundred and fiftieth anniversary of the Quincy church.

None of our oldest churches have inspired me with a profounder respect. It is not merely the eminent men whose names are indissolubly connected with it, nor my recollections of the sainted Lunt, — the only one of your pastors whom I much knew, — but quite as much the consistent spirit, the unity of purpose, which has run through its whole history, never locked up in an unprogressive theology, and never opening its doors to the vagaries of radicalism.

As I pass in the train through your new city I never need the shining dome on your church to remind me of the historical glory that covers that temple.

I am slowly recovering from a protracted illness, and have as yet gone only a few rods from my house. It will be impossible for me to be with you on the 29th instant, and I can only send to you my heartiest and best wishes.

Very cordially yours,

HENRY A. MILES.

FROM JOHN QUINCY ADAMS.

DEAR SIR, — It will be a great gratification to me to attend the delivery of your occasional discourse on Sunday the 22d, and an equal disappointment that by reason of an engagement already entered into to spend the 29th at Wareham, I shall not be able to be present at the celebration.

Yours truly, J. Q. ADAMS.

SEPT. 21, 1889.

THE ADAMS MANSION.

CORNER IN THE DRAWING ROOM OF THE ADAMS MANSION

FROM THE PILGRIMS' CHURCH AT PLYMOUTH.

PLYMOUTH, MASS., Sept. 26, 1889.

Mr. LEWIS BASS, Quincy, Mass.

DEAR SIR, — It is with regret that I am compelled to decline the invitation to be present at the services of commemoration to be held in the First Church in Quincy on Sunday next.

The duties of my own pulpit require my presence here.

The First Parish in Plymouth sends greeting and congratulations to her younger sister, with best wishes for continued prosperity.

Sincerely yours,

CHAS. P. LOMBARD.

FROM THE REV. R. C. WATERSTON.

MOUNTAIN COTTAGE, WHITEFIELD, N. H.,
Sept. 20, 1889.

LEWIS BASS, Esq.

DEAR SIR, — I desire through you to acknowledge with thanks your kind invitation to attend the two hundred and fiftieth anniversary of the First Church of Quincy, — an occasion of sacred interest and which must be in every respect a most memorable occasion.

Nothing could give me greater pleasure than to participate in such a commemoration; but I exceedingly regret that the condition of my health is such as to render it impossible. In thought and in spirit I shall be with you, cherishing with you grateful remembrance of those remarkable and illustrious men who have gone forth from that church to fill with honor the most responsible stations in the gift of their country, and to leave behind them names which the nation and the world delight — as ever will delight — to hold in the highest veneration and gratitude. While they were beloved by the church, they were also the benefactors both of their country and the world. The associations awakened by such a commemoration must inevitably strike their roots deep, and spread their influences far and wide.

No church, I cannot but think, on this whole continent, has reason to cherish with such gratitude the memories of the past.

To be present at such a commemoration would be the greatest possible privilege, which nothing but the condition of my health could cause me to forego. With many thanks for your kind remembrance,

I am, most respectfully and sincerely, yours,

R. C. WATERSTON.

FROM THE REV. G. M. BARTOL.

LANCASTER, MASS., Sept. 27, 1889.

Mr. LEWIS BASS, Quincy.

DEAR SIR, — The invitation of the First Church of Quincy, by its committee, for the 29th instant, was received with unusual pleasure.

Any retrospect of the two hundred and fifty years now so near completion must be a gratifying one, bearing witness to repeated and successful efforts for the extension of civil, religious, and industrial freedom, of just and humane principles, and of knowledge and intelligence among the mass of the people by improved methods of instruction and the multiplication of free libraries. In the promotion of all these ends a long line of good and wise and faithful men connected with your religious society have borne a noteworthy share. And surely it is well that the chain which unites its coming anniversary with the memories of what they were and what they have done should be strengthened and brightened, as it will be, by your proposed observance.

Any commemoration which makes the past predominate over

the present and the future, or which makes more of the date of an event than of the event itself, — forgetting that there is no such thing as the precise fixing of a date, because no almanac of ours can give us a perfect measure of time, — is false and superstitious; but a commemoration which associates the particular occasion with events that illustrate important principles, is legitimate, and wholesome in its effects. It inculcates those principles more forcibly upon us. It makes us feel the unity of the past with the present, and of the present with the future, the unity of all being, and the unity of all portions of the great providential plan which is ever working out the purposes for which we were placed where we are.

Be pleased to accept herewith an assurance of our cordial thanks for your thoughtful remembrance of the First Church of Lancaster. I am sorry to be obliged to add my sincere regret in finding that other engagements must prevent me from availing myself of a privilege which I should so highly esteem.

With earnest desires that the occasion may prove as pleasant and profitable to all interested as you yourselves can wish,

Very respectfully and truly,

GEORGE M. BARTOL.

FROM THE HON. JOHN D. LONG.

BOSTON, Sept. 18, 1889.

DEAR MR. WILSON, — I regret very much that I cannot avail myself of your very kind invitation to the church commemoration at Quincy on the 29th; but I expect to be away on that Sunday, and my engagements are such that I cannot change them. It will certainly be a memorable occasion, and I send my most cordial good wishes.

Very truly yours,

JOHN D. LONG.

Rev. D. M. WILSON, Quincy.

FROM THE REV. JOHN CORDNER, D.D.

BOSTON, Sept. 18, 1889.

Mr. LEWIS BASS.

DEAR SIR, — Many thanks to your committee for the courtesy of an invitation to your proposed commemoration September 29. The First Church, Quincy, has an honorable record, and has had in the past, as it has in the present, names eminent in public and private life. It would be to me a great pleasure to be with you on an occasion so interesting; but I feel that I must deny myself. The state of my health just now compels me, much to my regret, to decline your very kind invitation.

Truly yours,

JOHN CORDNER.

FROM THE REV. GEORGE S. BALL.

UPTON, Sept. 18, 1889.

To the Committee on Invitations to attend the Services in Commemoration of the Completion of Two Hundred and Fifty Years of the First Church in Quincy.

GENTLEMEN, — I thank you most heartily for your cordial invitation to be present at the two hundred and fiftieth anniversary services of your church. It has a most marked history, and one well worthy commemoration. The ministers and laymen of it have been distinguished for scholarship and statesmanship, — for ability, piety, and public influence.

During the ministry of that marked scholar and eloquent preacher, Rev. William P. Lunt, whose death was such a loss to your church and the community at large, I became somewhat interested in the society and acquainted with its history. Mr. Lunt quite frequently exchanged pulpits with me, to the great delight of my people at Plymouth. To me the opportunity to hear him preach was a very great pleasure, and in his most inspired moments he impressed me as among the great pulpit orators. Your invitation and anniversary recall these days before the war.

I am also interested anew by dear friends who are now members of your parish, and deeply regret a combination of circumstances which, I fear, will prevent me from being present as I desire to be.

I know it must be a deeply interesting occasion. May it also be a profitable one, coming to you as an inspiration for fuller life as the years go by.

In the bonds of fellowship,

I am most truly yours, GEO. S. BALL.

FROM THE REV. GEORGE A. THAYER.

CINCINNATI, Sept. 18, 1889.

LEWIS BASS, Esq.

MY DEAR SIR, — I should be very glad if just at this time I could be a resident of some town nearer Quincy than is my Ohio home, that I might join in the celebration to which you kindly invite me, of your two hundred and fiftieth church anniversary. But a thousand miles is not easily traversed in a busy season, and I must be content to rejoice in the spirit with your people over what, to a dweller in one of the newer sections of a comparatively youthful and recent republic, seems an exceeding venerable age, — an age which does not consist solely in number of years, but in honorable service to all the higher interests of the community in which the church has lived. To an institution as well as to an individual the words of the book of "Wisdom" apply: "Honorable age is not that which standeth in length of time, . . . but wisdom is the gray hair, and an unspotted life is old age." And such maturity certainly belongs to the career of excellent service for God and for man of which your people are about to take a retrospect.

Very truly yours, GEORGE A. THAYER.

FROM THE REV. CHARLES NOYES.

NORTH ANDOVER, Sept. 25, 1889.

Mr. LEWIS BASS.

DEAR SIR, — It would give me great pleasure to attend the services of the First Church, Quincy, in commemoration of its completion of two hundred and fifty years. My pulpit duties at North Andover on September 29 will not, however, allow me to be present.

I regret this the more because I was once honored with an invitation to become pastor of the First Church, and have followed with special interest the record of its welfare and prosperity. May its future history tell of as faithful services to the cause of truth and righteousness as does that of the past two hundred and fifty years.

Truly your friend,

CHARLES NOYES.

FROM SAMUEL A. BATES.

SOUTH BRAINTREE, Sept. 20, 1889.

Messrs. ADAMS, BASS, DEWSON, and FAXON, Committee of First Church, Quincy, Mass.

MANY thanks for your kind invitation to the two hundred and fiftieth anniversary of your church. If nothing prevents, I shall be present on that occasion to enjoy with you the rehearsal of the noble deeds of our fathers who established on our soil the principles which have in the past governed the nation, and which I trust in the future will guide its destinies with success. May success attend your efforts in endeavoring to throw light upon the past history of your church, and of keeping the acts of those sires green in our memories! Again thanking you for your kind invitation,

I remain yours truly,

SAMUEL A. BATES.

FROM MRS. F. AUGUSTUS WHITNEY.

ALLSTON, Sept. 19, 1889.

MRS. F. AUGUSTUS WHITNEY, in acknowledging the cordial invitation of the committee to the commemorative services of the First Church in Quincy, feels great regret that illness will prevent her being present on an occasion in which she feels deep interest as being associated with the society so closely identified with the early interests of her late husband and of his family.

FROM THE REV. A. B. MUZZEY.

CAMBRIDGE, Sept. 20, 1889.

THE First Church, Quincy, the parent and home of great men, nationally, intellectually, and spiritually, and so honored in its long history, does wisely and justly in commemorating its two hundred and fiftieth anniversary by special services.

For these reasons, and drawn also toward your church as I am by personal relations and associations, I accept with peculiar pleasure their cordial invitation, and although eighty-seven years of age, trust nothing will prevent my attendance.

ARTEMAS B. MUZZEY.

FROM SELECTMEN OF TOWNS IN OLD BRAINTREE.

HOLBROOK, MASS., September, 1889.

Mr. LEWIS BASS.

DEAR SIR, — Your invitation for the 29th is received, for which accept our thanks. We will endeavor to be present.

Yours,

ABRAM C. HOLBROOK,
Chairman of Selectmen.

LEWIS BASS, Esq.

RANDOLPH, MASS., Sept. 20, 1889.

DEAR SIR, — Your invitation to selectmen to attend the services in commemoration of the completion of the two hundred and fifty years of the First Church, Quincy, has come to hand, and the selectmen have voted to accept the invitation and be present at the services. With many thanks for the invitation,

I am yours respectfully,

MICHAEL J. DALY,
Secretary of Selectmen.

Mr. BASS.

BRAINTREE, Sept. 23, 1889.

YOUR invitation to attend the two hundred and fiftieth anniversary of the formation of the First Church is received, and thanking you for the same, will be pleased to attend.

NATHANIEL F. HUNT,
For the Selectmen of the Town of Braintree.

FROM THE REV. S. H. WINKLEY.

Mr. LEWIS BASS.

BOSTON, Sept. 18, 1889.

DEAR SIR, — Permit me through you to thank the committee for its kind invitation to be present at the coming two hundred and fiftieth anniversary of the First Church in Quincy. I have two services for that afternoon, which will prevent my accepting the same. What a grand history that church has! And what names inscribed upon its roll! May its future be even more successful than its past!

Regretfully,

S. H. WINKLEY.

FROM THE REV. EDWARD H. HALL.

CAMBRIDGE, Sept. 20, 1889.

MY DEAR MR. WILSON, — I have just received your note and the official invitation to your anniversary, and feel of course the greatest interest in the celebration. It seems like a continuation of our own three years ago, and I should be extremely sorry not to have our church represented. Unfortunately, however, it will be quite impossible for me to get over in time for the entire exercises, even if I can get to you at all. I have a meeting immediately after the morning service which will prevent my reaching the 1.30 train; and if I understand the time-table aright, there is no other train till 5, — which will be too late, I suppose, for any of the ceremonies. If it were possible, I would come in for what little I could get at the close. I need not say how much I regret this, as otherwise I should enjoy coming very much, and should do my best to say a few words of greeting. Hoping that the occasion will be an altogether successful one,

I am sincerely yours,

EDWARD H. HALL.

FROM THE REV. CRAWFORD NIGHTINGALE.

ASHMONT, DORCHESTER, Sept. 17, 1889.

DEAR SIR, — The card of invitation to the commemorative services at Quincy on the 29th instant was received with much pleasure. The occasion will have a special interest for me, as my ancestors for several generations were residents of "that part of Braintree now called Quincy." Among them was Joseph Nightingale, who married Hannah Bass, and who named as executors of his will "Samuel Sewell and Samuel Bass, his trusty friends and kinsmen, and John Adams."

Yours truly,

CRAWFORD NIGHTINGALE.

FROM THE OLD HINGHAM CHURCH.

HINGHAM, Sept. 23, 1889.

The First Parish in Hingham accepts with pleasure the invitation of the First Church, Quincy, to send representatives to its commemorative services, September 29, and has appointed four delegates for that purpose.

Cordially and respectfully yours,

EBED L. RIPLEY,
Chairman of the Committee of the First Parish in Hingham.

FROM HARRISON J. DAWES.

NEWTON CENTRE, Sept. 20, 1889.

Mr. LEWIS BASS.

DEAR SIR, — I am very sorry to be obliged to decline the invitation to be present at the two hundred and fiftieth anniversary of the founding of our church. My health does not permit of my going out. In behalf of the Committee on Invitation please accept my regrets, and also my heartfelt good wishes for the continued prosperity of the society.

Respectfully,

HARRISON J. DAWES.

FROM THE REV. EDWIN DAVIS.

ORANGE, MASS., Sept. 27, 1889.

Mr. BASS.

DEAR SIR, — I wish gratefully to acknowledge the receipt of a very kind invitation from the committee who have the matter in charge to attend the celebration of the two hundred and fiftieth anniversary of the formation of the First Congregational Parish in Quincy. I regret exceedingly that circumstances beyond my control compel me to be absent from town on the 29th instant, which were they otherwise would permit me to enjoy the pleasure of being present with you at that time. Be assured of my interest in the event, and accept the assurance that "though absent in body, I am present in spirit." Thanking the Committee for their kind invitation,

I am, fraternally yours,
EDWIN DAVIS.

FROM THE REV. F. FROTHINGHAM.

OLD ORCHARD, ME., Sept. 26, 1889.

Mr. LEWIS BASS, Quincy, Mass.

MY DEAR SIR, — I beg you to accept my thanks for your kind invitation on behalf of the First Church of Quincy to the celebration of its two hundred and fiftieth anniversary. How gladly would I be present to share in the memories and associations of an occasion so rich in both! But I am away from home, and must deny myself the privilege. But I cordially express the hope that the celebration of your anniversary may be not only full of good inspiration from the long past, but abound in good promise and augury for the longer and may it be the ever-improving and greatening future. With all good wishes,

I remain, dear sir, your and its friend and servant,
FREDK. FROTHINGHAM.

FROM GEORGE GREENLEAF DAWES.

BOSTON, Sept. 23, 1889.

Mr. LEWIS BASS.

DEAR SIR, — I received an invitation from the First Church of Quincy to be present at their two hundred and fiftieth anniversary. It will be impossible for me to be present; but I feel a great interest in the welfare of the church wherein I was reared, and where my ancestors for many generations have worshipped. Thanking you for remembering me,

I am very truly yours,
GEORGE GREENLEAF DAWES.

PRELIMINARY PROCEEDINGS.

AT the annual parish meeting, the 11th of March, 1889, the following named persons were appointed to make all arrangements for the proper celebration of the two hundred and fiftieth anniversary of the gathering of First Church : —

Rev. D. M. WILSON, CHARLES FRANCIS ADAMS,
EDWARD H. DEWSON, LEWIS BASS,
WILLIAM LYMAN FAXON, Mrs. WILLIAM B. RICE,
Mrs. WILSON TISDALE, Mrs. J. FRANKLIN FAXON,
Mrs. JOHN Q. A. FIELD, Mrs. THOMAS A. WHICHER.

A meeting of this committee was held soon afterward. The pastor acted as chairman, and Mr. Lewis Bass was chosen secretary. It was decided to have the commemorative services on the afternoon of Sunday, the 29th of September, 1889, and to invite several gentlemen to deliver addresses. The pastor announced that he would preach two introductory sermons, — one on the morning of September 22, and the other on the morning of September 29. The following sub-committees were then appointed to carry out the arrangements in detail : —

Committee on Invitations.

Mr. CHARLES FRANCIS ADAMS, Mr. EDWARD H. DEWSON,
Mr. LEWIS BASS, Mr. WILLIAM LYMAN FAXON.

On Programme.

Rev. D. MUNRO WILSON, Mr. L. H. H. JOHNSON,
Mr. HARRY L. RICE.

On Reception of Guests.

Mr. EDWARD H. DEWSON, Mr. CHARLES A. HOWLAND,
Mr. GEORGE L. GILL, Mr. JOHN Q. A. FIELD,
Mr. JOSEPH L. WHITON, Mr. FRANK B. FOSTER,
Mr. J. HENRY EMERY, Mrs. J. FRANKLIN FAXON,
Mr. JOSEPH C. MORSE, Mrs. LEWIS BASS,
Mrs. JOHN O. HOLDEN.

On Decorations.

Mr. FRED B. RICE, Mrs. GEORGE B. WENDELL,
Mr. EDWARD WHICHER, Mrs. EBEN C. STANWOOD,
Mr. WILLIAM I. DEWSON, Mrs. GEORGE L. KEYES,
Mrs. WILLIAM B. RICE, Miss MINNIE J. PRATT.

On Music.

Mr. WILLIAM B. RICE, Mr. JOHN SHAW, JR.,
Mr. GEORGE H. FIELD, Mrs. WILSON TISDALE,
Mr. HENRY M. FAXON, Mrs. HORACE F. SPEAR,
Miss ABBY C. CHAMBERLIN.

On Refreshments.

Mrs. THOMAS A. WHICHER, Mrs. RUFUS FOSTER,
Mrs. JOHN Q. A. FIELD, Mrs. IBRAHIM MORRISON,
Mrs. JAMES H. STETSON, Mrs. GEORGE W. MORTON,
Mrs. M. A. PERKINS, Mrs. SAMUEL CRANE,
Mrs. JAMES H. SLADE, Mrs. EUGENE N. HULTMAN.

On Finance.

Mr. HENRY H. FAXON, Mr. CHARLES H. PORTER,
Mr. EDWIN B. PRATT, Mr. J. FRANKLIN FAXON,
Mr. JAMES EDWARDS, Mr. LUTHER S. ANDERSON.

OUR QUARTO-MILLENNIAL CHOIR.

WILLIAM B. RICE, *Leader.*   ABBY C. CHAMBERLIN, *Organist.*

Sopranos.

Mrs. HORACE F. SPEAR,   Miss MAY MCPHAIL,
Miss MINNIE W. LITCHFIELD,   Miss S. ELIZABETH ACKERMAN,
Mrs. CYRUS T. SHERMAN,   Miss GRACE ISAACS,
Miss LAURA HAYWARD.

Tenors.

JAMES F. HARLOW,   WALTER M. PACKARD,
GEORGE HARVEY FIELD.

Altos.

Mrs. GEORGE HARVEY FIELD,   Miss MARY GARDNER,
Mrs. WALTER M. PACKARD,   Mrs. WILLIAM AUSTIN WINSLOW,
Miss LILLIE TABER,   Miss LILLIE SCAMMELL.

Basses.

PETER B. GOMEZ,   GEORGE ARTHUR SHERMAN,
CHARLES H. PORTER, JR.,   J. FRANKLIN BURRELL,
CYRUS T. SHERMAN.

APPENDIX.

THE COVENANT.

THE following is the original Covenant which was presented when the Church was gathered, and then signed by the two ministers and six others. The Rev. John Hancock printed it with his sermons preached at the close of the first century of our Church's existence: —

"We poor unworthy creatures, who have sometime lived without Christ and without God in the world, and so have deserved rather fellowship with the devil and his angels than with God and his saints, being called of God out of this world to the fellowship of Christ by the Ministry of the Gospel, and our hearts made willing to join together in Church Fellowship, so by the help and strength of Christ, renounce the devil, the wicked world, a sinful flesh, with all the remnants of Anti-Christian pollution wherein sometimes we have walked, and all our former evil ways, and do give up ourselves, first to God the Father, Son, and Holy Ghost, and offer up our proffered subjection to our Lord Jesus Christ as the only Priest, Prophet and King of his Church, beseeching him in his rich grace and free mercy to accept us for his people in the blood of his Covenant; and we give up ourselves also one to another by the will of God, promising in the name and power of our Lord Jesus Christ, who worketh in us both to will and to do according to his good pleasure, to worship the Lord in Spirit and Truth, and to walk in brotherly love and the duties thereof according to the will of the Gospel, to the edification of the body and of each member therein, and to be guided in all things according to God's revealed will, seeking to advance the Glory of Jesus Christ, our head, both in Church and Brotherly Communion, thro' the assistance of his Holy Spirit which he hath promised to his Church; and we do manifest our joint consent herein this day in presence of this assembly, by this our present public profession, and by giving to one another the right hand of fellowship.

"WM. TOMPSON, Pastor.   JOHN DASSETT.
HENRY FLYNT, Teacher.   WILLIAM POTTER.
GEORGE ROSE.   MARTIN SAUNDERS.
STEPHEN KINSLEY, Elder.   GREGORY BELCHER."

THE DEACONS.

SAMUEL BASS,	July 5, 1640,	Received to Communion.
ALEXANDER WINCHESTER,	" 12, "	Dismissed from Boston Church.
RICHARD BRACKETT,	" 21, 1642,	" " " "
FRANCIS ELIOT,	Oct. 12, 1653.	
WILLIAM ALICE,	" " "	
ROBERT PARMENTER,	Nov. 2, 1679.	
SAMUEL TOMPSON,	" " "	
THOMAS BASS.		
JOSEPH PENNIMAN.		
NATHANIEL WALES.		
BENJAMIN SAVIL.		
MOSES PAINE.		
GREGORY BELCHER.		
PETER ADAMS,	Aug. 21, 1727.	
SAMUEL SAVIL,	" " "	
JONATHAN WEBB,	May 11, 1747.	
JOHN ADAMS,	" " "	
JOSEPH PALMER,	" 29, 1752.	
MOSES BELCHER,	" " "	
JOSEPH NEAL, JR.,	" " "	
DANIEL ARNOLD,	" 3, 1769.	
BENJAMIN BASS,	" 1, 1771.	
EBENEZER ADAMS,	Nov. 3, 1773.	
JONATHAN WEBB.		
ELIJAH VEAZIE.		
JONATHAN BASS.		
JOSIAH ADAMS.		
DANIEL SPEAR,	Jan. 27, 1811.	
SAMUEL SAVIL,	Oct. 24, 1817.	
WILLIAM SPEAR,	Nov. 22, 1835.	
JAMES NEWCOMB,	" " "	
ELIJAH BAXTER,	April 4, 1844.	Died Feb. 2, 1868.
GEORGE BAXTER,	July 21, "	" Dec. 14, 1870.
THOMAS G. FENNO,	Jan. 20, 1861.	" Jan. 11, 1865.

MEETING-HOUSES.

It was the making repairs much needed in the old stone meeting-house which opened the way for the introduction of the pew system, as the following vote indicates: —

"OCTOBER 22, 1697.

"*Voted* at the same time that upon the drawing up or uniting the men's seats with the women's in the present alley, any Roome being left after alterations in the meeting-house, any person with consent of the Committee Selectmen may at their own proper charges mak pews for themselves and familys." (Braintree Records, p. 36.)

Then it was that the aspiring person spoken of in the second discourse asked permission to build the pew over the pulpit. Seats at this time must have been very scarce in the meeting-house, every available place occupied, to lead the respectable Mr. Rawson to make this cherubic exhibition of himself and the members of his household. One would give much to see them soberly seated up there above the dignified deacons, and right over the didactic minister Fiske. Here is the vote: —

"OCTOBER 22, 1697.

"*Voted* also at the same time that Mr William Rawson should have priviledge of making a seate for his familie, between or upon the two beams over the pulpit, not darkening the pulpit." (Braintree Records, p. 36.)

For ten years or so Mr. Rawson and his family looked down upon his fellow-worshippers and his minister; then, in 1709, it was voted "that Mr William Rawson sen^r shall have the Liberty of a Pew on the back side of the meeting-house for himself and all his Family at the left hand of Mr Wilson's Pew, Mr Wilson's and Mr Quinsey's Pews being removed back to ye wall." But it was a standing difficulty to dispose of Mr. Rawson. Two votes more, one in 1710 and the other in 1711, were taken before he was finally seated in "a second Pew home to the wall, at the west end of the meeting-house."

These pews, by the way, were granted with the most liberal conditions. Captain Wilson, who was the first to obtain permission to build one, was allowed to put it in whatever convenient place he should elect, and Joseph Crosby, to secure room enough for his, was granted leave to move the east door about four feet to the northward. To do this, he stoned up the old door, and then tore down the wall to make the new door. Although those of the "south end" had withdrawn, the floor was soon covered with seats and pews, and then David Bass thought he discovered a vacant spot by the east window where a pew might be squeezed in, and applied for the space. But this was too much crowding even for the men of those days, and accordingly the vote passed in the negative. The passion for exclusiveness also got possession of John Sanders and Samuel Savel, and it was voted they "should have the Two hindermost short seats in the gallery, in the southwest side of the meeting-house extending to the Beams, for a Pew for their wives and children." Aristocracy and exclusiveness might have dominion on the ground floor; but in the gallery, — no! the boys were there, the tireless baiters of tithingmen. When Sanders and Company came one Sunday to occupy their new pew, they found it a wreck. Some five months after they had obtained the coveted privilege, "it was put by the Moderator whether they would Relinquish their Right to their Pew, which was broken, to the Precinct. They then did both thereupon Resign their Right to ye Precinct." No second attempt, I believe, was made to build a pew in the galleries.

I have tried to make a plan of this old church after the pews were all arranged in it, and think I have been fairly successful. The building was so nearly square that the same wall was sometimes called a side and sometimes an end. So I have assumed it was thirty-five feet square. The pews can be placed with tolerable accuracy; they could be placed with entire accuracy if one could be sure where the stairs to the women's gallery were situated. I have drawn them in the northwest corner; they may have been in the southwest corner. But after all it is only a matter of the order of the pews against the west wall, — they being described as first from the women's stairs, second from the women's stairs, etc. It is to be taken into consideration, however, that seats and pews were placed with no such regularity

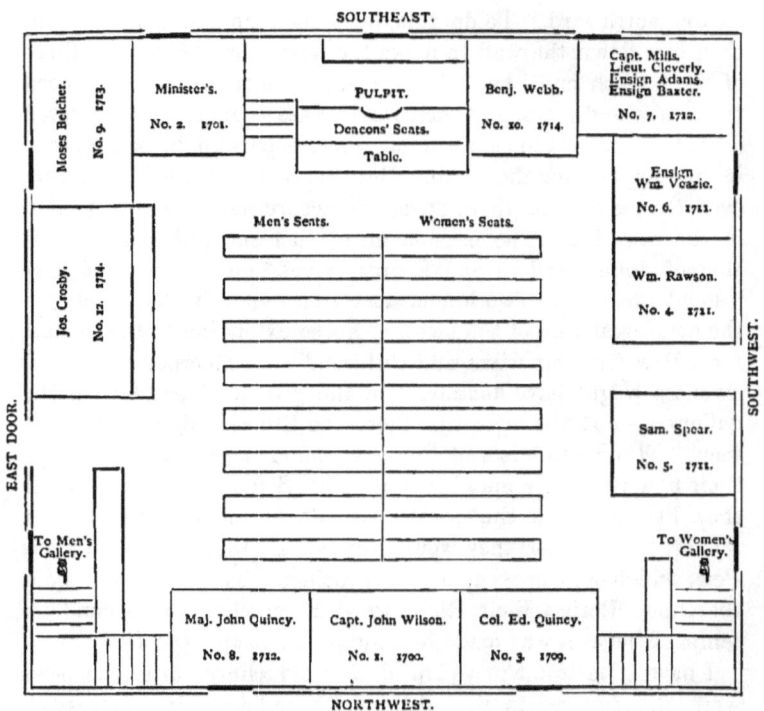

and symmetry as would appear by the plan. The figures indicate the order and the year in which the pews were built. An opening is left for a west door, but I am not sure that there was one.

The old stone meeting-house, unused and dismantled of belfry and windows, was permitted to stand in the little town common till 1747, when it was sold at auction to Serg. Moses Belcher and Mr. Joseph Nightingale for £100, old tenor. At one time it was proposed to convert it into a poor-house, but upon consideration it was found not to be easily adapted to that use.

Hancock's meeting-house was sixty feet in length by forty feet in width (inside measurement). The committee chosen to build it "were Col. Edmund Quincey, Major John Quincey, Lieut. Joseph Neall, Mr. Benjamin Beall, Deacon Peter Adams, Ensign Samuel Baxter, and Mr. Joseph Crosbey." "Then the question was asked whether the said house should be accomidated with Pews as conveniently as may be, it passed in the affirmative." Pews were still such an innovation that it was not to be taken for granted they would be built in the new meeting-house; and the vote to have them is not to be taken as implying that the entire floor and the galleries were to be occupied by them, as in modern churches. The half-way system in vogue in the later years of the old stone edifice was carried over into the new building. The floor, for the most part, was still to be covered with the two rows of the "men's seats" and the "women's seats," and the front of the galleries was reserved, the south one for the women, the north one for the men. Thus the pews were mainly set against the walls. They were of the little-square-room description, and were disposed of in five lots, as follows: "eight pews at £25, twelve at £15, eight at £12, six at £10, and six at £7, and in the galleries twenty pews, viz., eight in the front against the wall at £10; and (if it be thought convenient) six on each side (against the wall) at £8." John Adams, afterwards deacon, was the clerk at this time, and he records an "account of the persons who drew pews in the new meeting-house, and of the situation of the said pews as the same were drawn persuant to a rule agreed upon for that end the fourteenth day of August, 1732." It is from that account and other minutes that the diagram under the picture of the church on a preceding page is made. Pews in the galleries at about the same time were also disposed of to the following persons: Lieut. Thomas Crosby, Deacon Samuel Savel, Samuel Adams, Nathaniel Gilbird, Joseph Crosby, Jr., Aaron Hayward, Thomas Cleverly, William Hayden, Jr., Ezekiel Crane. On a higher level still Capt. Samuel Baxter built him a pew above the women's stairs in the gallery, and Lieut. Joseph Crosbey was granted the similar place above the men's stairs. In time, more pews were built on the ground floor, usurping the place of the benches, and the remaining benches were joined together in some places across the aisle, and short seats put up where any room was to be had, so that at last only those expert at it could thread the devious path among them. From the memoirs of the wife of President Quincy (she came here in 1798) the following view of the interior of the church at a later time is obtained:—

"The pews in the centre . . . having been made out of long open seats, by successive votes of the town, were of different sizes, and had no regularity of arrangement, and several were entered by narrow passages, winding between those in their neighborhood. The seats being provided with hinges were raised when the congregation stood during the prayer, and at its conclusion thrown down with a momentum which on her first attendance alarmed Mrs. Quincy, who feared the church was falling. The deacons were ranged under the pulpit, and beside its door the sexton was seated, while from an aparture aloft in the wall the bell-ringer looked in from the tower to mark the arrival of the clergyman. The voices of the choir in the front gallery were assisted by a discordant assemblage of stringed and wind instruments."

Not altogether by the "poorer sort" were the "seats" occupied. Very many of the most respectable people in the parish filled them. Here is a record in illustration: "Whare as Mrs. Mary Norton hath of late given to Braintree North Precinct a Velvet Cushen of Considerable Value. Voted, that thanks be Returned to the said Madm. Norton for the Gift aforesaid, and that she be invited to tak the upper end of the fore seet for her seet in the new Meeting-House." It was on these "fore seets" that John Adams as a boy saw from his father's pew near the pulpit those rows of "venerable heads," a sight which affected him deeply. The invasions began to be made upon the seats, when on April 4th, 1757, it was voted, "That the Ground upon wch the two hindermost seats on each side the Midle Alley Stand Be Disposed of in order that Pues may Be rested their on by ye Purchers, provided four appear for that porpus." The expected "Purchers" were of those who sat on the seats; the discomfort suggested in the word "Purchers" is not intentional, but, sitting in our luxurious modern pews, we may regard it as a "palpable hit."

The choir came into existence in March, 1764. The following is a vote recorded at that time: "That the two seats in the front Gallery Be Divided By an Alle in the Midle of Sd seats To acomidate those persons that have Ben att Pains and expense to Gain Instruction in the Use of Psalmody, and that the Division next the Womans Seets Be their Part." In 1772 they were invited to "acomidate" themselves below, where the "men's hind seats" and the "women's hind seats" are "now standing," and in 1794 they were coaxed back into the gallery again.

In 1805 the church was enlarged "by sawing the building lengthwise with the ridge pole, from north to South, moving the front, or west portion of the same, fifteen feet forward, and framing in the intermediate space." A little before this the stairs to the galleries in both the west corners were removed, and entrances to the galleries effected by the tower on the north side, and by a tall porch on the south side. The ground floor of the church as thus altered, and as it appeared when the building was taken down, in 1828, was represented in the Rev. George Whitney's History of Quincy. This we print, not only because it shows us the plan of the pews, but also because it shows us who were the members of the parish at this time, and how they disposed themselves (see page 145).

To make the list of pew-owners complete, we add those who held pews in the galleries: Bryant Newcomb, Capt. Benjamin Page, Alpheus and Lemuel Spear one pew between them, George

APPENDIX. 145

Spear, Ebenezer Bent, Thomas Adams, Solomon and Josiah Nightingale one, Ezra Glover, Daniel Spear. "The first four pews," says Mr. Whitney, "were in the east end of the south

			EAST. 61 feet.					
Dwelt and H. Wood. 83	Spear. 84	Beale. 85	Adams and Turner. 86	Town's Poor. 87	Pulpit. / Deacons' Seat. Table.	Spear. 49	Raw- son. 50	Deacon Adams. 51	Bass and Seaver. 52	Crane & Nightingale. 53	Brackett. 54
Billings 82		48 Gen. Taylor.	Ministry. 24		1 Presidents.	Baxter. 25		55 J. Brac- kett.
Dea. Vensie. 81		47 Glover.	Baxter. 23		2 Greenleaf.	Den. Spear & N. Bent. 26		56 Dr. Phipps.
Cooke. 80		46 Fenno.	Mayo. 22		3 Nightingale	Baxter. 27		57 L. Baxter.
		45 Glover.	Jenkins. 21		4 Tufts.	Newcomb. 28		
Hard- wick. 79		44 Hall.	Thayer & Brigham. 20		5 Riddle.	Curtis. 29		58 H. Hard- wick.
Stove.		43 Souther.	Capt. Bass. 19		6 Baxter.	Curtis. 30		
		42 Savil.	Judge Greenleaf 18		7 Judge Adams.	Deacon Savil. 31		
Night- ingale. 78		41 Pope.	S. Spear. 17		8 Briesler.	Crane & Nightingale. 32		65 Keat- ing.
T. Adams 77		40 Green.	Beale. 16		9 Miller.	Baxter & Wild. 33		66 MR&E Marsh.
J. Marsh. 76		39 Apthorp.	E. Spear. 15		10 Quincy.	Quincy. 34		67 W. Marsh.
		38 Appleton.	Willett & French. 14		11 Shaw & Chubbuck.	Hardwick. 35		
Glover, N. & H. 75		37 Billings.	Brackett & Newcomb. 13		12 B. & J. Faxon	Bass. 36		68 W New- comb.
Bick- nell. 74								69 Pray.
	73 W. Wood & Crane.	72 Billings and Faxon	71 P. Brac- kett	70 Judge Cranch & J. Greenleaf	89 Deacon and L. Bass.	88 E. Adams and J. Whitney.	87 W. Spear and Hobart.	86 T. Adams.	59 Field & W. Baxter.

GROUND FLOOR AFTER THE ALTERATIONS OF THE BUILDING IN 1805.

gallery, and were occupied by the owners. The others were on the back of the west gallery, most of the owners occupying their pews below."

It is instructive to know how this same congregation seated itself in the Stone Temple when it was ready for worship, in 1828, and we append a diagram made at that time (see page 146).

It would be a complete presentation of pew-owners if to the above plan could be added a plan of the galleries. No such plan, however, is to be found. I wrote to a lady, familiar all her days with the church and its people, with regard to the occupants of the galleries, and received this for answer: "I can only

10

APPENDIX.

PEWS IN THE NEW STONE MEETING-HOUSE, QUINCY.
134 ON THE FLOOR, 22 IN THE GALLERIES.

Gallery (top row, left to right):
126 Lem. Brackett. | 127 Eben. Adams. | 128 | 129 Asa Pope. | 130 Peter Turner. | 131 | 132 Peter Bicknell | 133 | 134 Luther Spear. | PULPIT. | 1 J. Q. Adams. | 2 J. Q. Adams. | 3 John Spear. | 4 John Bass. | 5 | 6 | 7 Dea. J. Adams. | 8 Nathl. Wilde. | 9 John Whicher.

125 Tho. Adams.	87 J. Whitemore.	86 Parish.	49 Capt. J. Whitney.	48 Wm. Baxter.	10 Wm. Baxter, Jr.
124 Capt. Batcheldor.	88 Isaac Bass.	85 Sam. Copland.	50 D. Greenleaf.	47 Dea. D. Spear.	11 James Baxter.
123 S. Littlefield.	89 E. W. Sampson.	84 Gen. T. Taylor.	51 Hon. T. Greenleaf	46 N. Curtis.	12 A. Willett.
122 Harvey Field.	90 Isaac Riddle.	83 Harvey Field.	52 E. Miller.	45 Cotton Tufts.	13 S. Nightingale.
121 Elisha Marsh.	91 Dea. S. Savil.	82 J. Williams.	53 Geo. W. Beale.	44 Josiah Nightingale.	14 Paul Wilde.
120 J. Brigham.	92 Ezra Glover.	81 Nath. White.	54 Hon. J. Q. Adams.	43 James Newcomb.	15 J. Briesler, Jr.
119 D. French.	93 Lem. Pope.	80 Adam Curtis.	55 Hon. J. Quincy.	42 Mrs. Baxter.	16 Wm. Wood.
118 P. Turner.	94 J. Bass, Jr.	79 Henry Wood.	56 Hon. J. Quincy.	41 Tho. B. Adams.	17 Doct. T. Phipps.
117 Mrs. Fenno	95 Hor. Glover.	78 Capt. J. Bass.	57 John Souther.	40 F. Hardwick.	18 James Edwards.
116 Capt. B. Page.	96 John Savil.	77 N. Josselyn.	58 J. Brigham.	39 Elijah Spear.	19 John Glover, Jr.
115 Josiah Savil.	97 John L. Souther.	76 Elihu Arnold.	59 Capt. O. Jenkins.	38 Elisha Marsh.	20 T. J. Nightingale.
114 L. Baxter.	98 A. Hardwick.	75	60 Eben. Shaw.	37 Josiah Hayden.	21 Tho. Nottage.
113 Tho. Taylor.	99 Jos. Burrell.	74	61	36 Geo. Nightingale.	22 John Dwelle.
112 Jon. Marsh.	100 S. Spear & G. Baxter.	73	62	35 D. Hobart.	23 J. H. Bass.
111 J. Quincy.	101	72	63 John Shaw.	34 Jon. Spear.	24 Jesse Newcomb.
110 Wm. Kidder.	102 H. Hardwick.	71	64	33 Alph. Spear.	25 Wm. Spear.
109 D. Greenleaf.	103	70	65	32 Geo. W. Beale.	26 Capt. J Bass.
108	104 Tho. Taylor.	69	66	31	27 Eben. Adams.
107	105	68 C. & L. Faxon.	67 J. Whitney.	30	28
106					29

remember Mr. Bryant Newcomb, from the Neck, Miss Mary Jane Turner's grandfather, and Ned Seaver, who sat in the gallery opposite Temple Street. . . . I saw Mrs. Jerusha Hardwick last evening, and she thought there were not many in the galleries in those days." I am inclined to think this latter conclusion is to be accepted. It was then considered the proper thing to sit downstairs, and not many gallery-pews would be purchased while pews were to be obtained within the fashionable area. As will be seen by the plan, a great many pews remained unsold on the floor. President J. Q. Adams bought thirty of them for three thousand dollars.

The building committee of the Stone Temple was composed of the following gentlemen : Thomas Greenleaf (chairman), Noah Curtis, John Souther, Lemuel Brackett, and Daniel Spear.

GIFTS OF COMMUNION VESSELS.

The following is a list of the sacred vessels belonging to First Church, with the inscriptions they bear, and some facts about those who gave them : —

A small cup, having two handles, and marked on the bottom, —

JOANNAH YORKE,
1685
B C

James Yorke and Johanna his wife were among the earliest members of our church. According to the Braintree records, a son was born to them June 14, 1648. Afterward they removed to Stonington, Conn., where in 1666 James was made freeman.

In the letter-book of Samuel Sewall, Vol. I. p. 28, is the following entry : —

February the 20th, 168$\frac{4}{5}$. I Samuel Tomson, Deacon of the Church of Christ at Braintrey, have received of Sam. Sewall one silver Goblet to the value of fourty shillings in money; which is in full of a Legacy of fourty shillings bequeathed said church by Mrs. Joanna Yorke of Stonington, lately deceased. In witness whereof I have hereunto set my hand and seal the day and year first above written.

SAMEL TOMPSON [Sig.].

ELIZABETH LANE.
MARY KAY.

A small cup of the same form as the preceding, bearing a coat-of-arms on the surface and marked on the bottom, —

B C
—— 1699 ——

The side opposite the coat-of-arms is marked, " Gift of Edmund Quincy, Esq., to the First Church of Braintree, now Quincy, by will dated December 11th, 1697."

A small cup of the same form as the preceding, plain on the surface, with the following inscription: " Ye gift of Decon Samll bas, Wm Veasey, Jno. Ruggle, David Walesby, 1694."

A high cup marked below the rim, " The gift of William Needham to Brantry Church, 1688." William Needham was granted in 1639 a house-plot out of the little island beyond Coddington's brook.

A high cup marked, —

The *B* is for Brackett, and the *R* stands for Richard, and the *A* for Alice his wife. Richard Brackett was in Boston in 1632, and with his wife Alice was dismissed from Boston church to Braintree church, Dec. 5, 1641. He probably came here earlier, as in June, 1638, he was granted leave to sell house and garden in Boston. Richard died the 3d of March, 1690, aged eighty; Alice died the 3d of November, 1690, aged seventy-six. The cup was probably given as a memorial of both after their death.

A high cup marked, " The gift of Mrs. Mehetable Fisher to the First Church of Christ in Braintree, 1741." In the old cemetery in

APPENDIX. 149

Quincy is a gravestone with this inscription : " Here lies Buried ye Body of Mrs. Mehitable Fisher, wife of Mr. Josiah Fisher. She died May 18th, 1741, in the 78 year of her age."

A cup marked, "The gift of ye Hon'ble Edmund Quincy, Esq., to ye First Church in Braintree, Feb'y 23d, 1737–38."

A tankard marked, "The gift of the Hon'ble John Quincy, Esq., to the First Church of Christ in Braintree, 1767."

A tankard marked, "The gift of Mrs. Sarah Adams (Relict of Mr. Edward Adams, late of Milton) to the First Church in Braintree." There is no date added, but the church records fix the time Nov. 4, 1770.

Four large-sized flagons, marked as follows : " Presented by Daniel Greenleaf to the Congregational Church in Quincy, 1828."

Three plates, marked thus : " Presented to the First Congregational Church in Quincy, by Deacon Josiah Adams, Deacon Daniel Spear, and Deacon Samuel Savil, 1828."

A baptismal vase having this inscription : "Presented to the Congregational Church in the town of Quincy, by Mrs. Eliza Susan Quincy, 1828."

A small cup having two handles, and marked on one side, —

$$\begin{array}{c} T \\ P \ \square \ M \end{array}$$

with the following inscription below it : " To the First Unitarian Church of Quincy, from Quincy Tufts, Weymouth, July 4, 1872 ; " on opposite side, C T to Q T ; and on bottom, —

$$\begin{array}{c} T \\ P \ * \ M \end{array}$$

A tankard bearing a coat of arms, and on the bottom, —

$$\begin{array}{c} E \quad\ \ \ Q \\ \ \ \ to \\ L \quad\ \ \ T \end{array}$$

marked, "To the First Unitarian Church in Quincy, from Quincy Tufts, Weymouth, July 4, 1872."

OTHER GIFTS TO THE CHURCH.

The clock on the front of the singers' gallery was presented, it is said, by Madam Abigail Adams, wife of President Adams, Sr., and Madam Esther Black, widow of the late Moses Black, Esq. The Rev. Frederick A. Whitney, however, says nothing of this, and quotes the following from a book we have not been able to find: "Sept. 30, 1799. Voted, that the thanks of the town be returned to President Adams and Mr. Moses Black for the present to the town of a clock in the meeting-house." When this clock was transferred to Stone Temple, it was "voted to put a new dial and glass to" it.

The fine crimson curtain which adorns the wall back of the pulpit was given to the church by Miss Nancy Brackett.

The two volumes of Scriptures, used in the pulpit, contain the following: "To the Church and Congregational Society of the Town of Quincy, this Bible, for the use of the Sacred Desk, is respectfully presented by Josiah Quincy. Boston, Oct., 1808."

"New bound and divided into two volumes, Oct., 1828. Josiah Quincy."

Mr. Thomas Adams, who died Jan. 2, 1869, bequeathed to the church the sum of ten thousand dollars for the support of public worship.

After the death of the Hon. Charles Francis Adams, it was seen by certain minutes he had written that he had it in mind to add ten thousand dollars to the amount given by Thomas Adams. No provision for this was made in his will; but the family of Mr. Adams offered the society ten thousand dollars, provided the total sum of both gifts, twenty thousand dollars, should be safely preserved, and the income of it applied to the support of worship and the care of the church building and the grounds around it. The society accepted the gift with the provisions attached, and appointed Henry A. Johnson, Edward H. Dewson, and Charles H. Porter a board of trustees to receive and manage the fund.

Miss Sarah Vinal, who died in Quincy, May 20, 1881, aged 85, bequeathed to the society one thousand dollars. The income of this sum is used to pay any expenses of the society.

WHEELWRIGHT'S PORTRAIT, AND OTHER PORTRAITS AND PICTURES.

The original painting from which the portrait of John Wheelwright in this volume is taken, hangs in one of the rooms of the Secretary of State at the State House. My attention was called to it by Mr. Henry B. Wheelwright, a direct descendant of the first pastor of this church. I had it taken down, and together with Mr. A. C. Goodell, Jr., and Mr. David Pulsifer, thoroughly scrutinized it. There is no name anywhere on or about the picture, no direct evidence that it is the portrait of the Rev. John Wheelwright; but an inscription in dark letters, almost concealed in the dark paint of the background, indirectly points to Wheelwright as the subject of it. That inscription was partly cut off when at some time the canvas was reduced to fit a smaller frame. It is as follows : —

"Aetat]is Suæ 84
Anno D]omini 1677."

These dates correspond very closely with the age of Mr. Wheelwright. He was born, says Mr. Bell, in the early part of 1593 ; add eighty-four years to that, and it carries us to the year 1677, the year of the portrait. So far as I can ascertain, there is only one other minister, — the portrait is that of a minister, — to whose age these figures so nicely accord. Roger Conant was born in 1592-93, and died Nov. 19, 1679, aged eighty-seven years. At one time the name of John Higginson got attached somehow to the portrait, but as that minister was born as late as 1616 the figures plainly have no application to him. Jeremy Belknap, the historian of New Hampshire, presented what appears to be a copy of this painting to the American Antiquarian Society of Worcester. John Higginson's name was then upon it, and it is from this fact, I am given to understand, that the portrait came to be called that of John Higginson. Those like Mr. Goodell, Jr., and Dr. Edward Strong, who have given some attention to the matter, are inclined to think it a veritable portrait of Wheelwright. It used to hang in the Senate Chamber. Wheelwright in his later years was still a marked man, not only as having been "like Roger Williams or worse," but also as having been the honored guest of his friends the great Cromwell and "Harry" Vane when in 1657 he visited England, and in this relation being of some considerable service to the colony. Besides this, "his children and grandchildren had married very conspicuously in society, and there might have been a strong feeling to do the old man justice in his failing age," and pay him such little attention as having his portrait painted. From letters written me by Mr. Henry B. Wheelwright, I venture to abstract the following: —

"John Wheelwright was the only clergyman in the colony of the age named in the inscription at the date given as that of the painting of the portrait. That's all any one can say about it, as far as known outside of the family; but I am convinced from the anatomy of the face, old and withered as it is, and its strong resemblance about the mouth and cheeks to some of my kindred, that it is old 'Boanerges' himself. . . . I have learned the value of little things as *clews;* they have led me, Theseus-like, out of many a mystery. As far back as I can remember in my family, there has been a 'trick' in each generation of carrying the thumb. My grandfather lived to ninety-one, and always sat in his armchair with hands slightly clasped, and *both* thumbs turned upward *rigidly, in extenso.* So with others of us who turn up *one* thumb. It is entirely involuntary with us all; *I* am liable to it if *I* go to thinking intently. Now, in this picture there's the old parson, with his hand on his Bible and thumb rigidly turned up in the air, like three generations of us that I know of. This seems laughable, to be sure, but identity is often detected by slighter 'clews.'

"Mr. John Wheelwright entered Sidney-Sussex College, Cambridge, April 28, 1611, pensioner, — which means that he was a person of property sufficient to maintain him in good style. I took this myself from the original books of Sidney-Sussex last spring."

Wheelwright died at Salisbury, Mass., Nov. 15, 1679. The family device on the tomb in King's Chapel yard is "Spectemur agendo;" and this, his descendant my correspondent thinks, is an entirely appropriate and accurately descriptive motto.

To Mr. Harrison J. Dawes, a descendant of Richard Cranch and closely resembling him in his features, I am indebted for the portrait of that vigorous scholar and eminent citizen. The picture has enough individuality about it to warrant it a good likeness. Another descendant was the late Mr. Richard Greenleaf. He had the original from which the photograph was taken that was lent to me by Mr. Dawes.

The portraits of members of the Adams family are, with the exception of that of the Hon. Charles Francis Adams, from original paintings. In his "Figures of the Past" Josiah Quincy has a pleasant description of John Adams sitting to Gilbert Stuart for the portrait copied for this book. From the brush of that celebrated painter came also the likeness of Abigail Adams. The portrait of John Quincy Adams was painted by Copley, and that of Mrs. J. Q. Adams by an unknown artist. Some of the best work of W. M. Hunt is exhibited in the portrait of Mrs. Charles F. Adams. The heliotype of the Hon. Charles F. Adams is from a very accurate photograph.

It was an antiquarian motive which induced me to publish pictures of houses representative of old Braintree. Already we regret the loss of houses which, locally, are historical, — notably the Hancock house destroyed many years ago by fire, and the house in which ministers Fiske and Marsh lived, lately removed to the back of his land by Charles H. Spear, of Franklin Street, the present owner. This latter house Samuel Tompson sold to Fiske, July 12, 1672 (Suffolk Deeds, 13 : 37, Br. Rec. p. 11). Is this the house Parson Tompson lived in? The Webb house seemed to have the first claim to preservation, as it is a contemporary and neighbor of the oldest meeting-house of which we have any record. It faced the little town common where the meeting-house stood, and, as I surmise, was built parallel with that branch of the road which diverged to the east to pass around the meeting-house. It was "from the fence of Benjamin Webb, southerly" into the common fronting the east door of the meeting-house, that sheds were built to shelter the horses of " persons liveing remote " (Br. Rec. pp. 41, 66). It is the last of the old houses which were situated in this neighborhood. The land on which it stands is that parcel which Benjamin Tompson purchased of Thomas Bass about 1679 (Br. Rec. p. 19), and which, with the house upon it, was sold by "Benjamin Tompson, of the town of Roxborough, school-master, . . . with the free consent of Prudence his wife, . . . to Benjamin Webb, of the town of Brantrey, leather-dresser," Nov. 14, 1700 (Suffolk Deeds, folio 20, p. 489). Probably Tompson built it and lived in it while teaching in the little schoolhouse on the common.

The Ruggles house, now occupied by Miss E. C. Adams and Mr. Isaac Hull Adams, is one of the oldest in Quincy; it is the rear part, however, which is the ancient house. This is the house referred to in Braintree Records, p. 6, where in 1655 " ther is layd one footway to ly from the Rocke by George Ruggells over the fresh Brooke." The "rocke" is still a marked object at the Elm Street end of the "Miller's style" path, which is the way then laid out. George Ruggells is living in Braintree in 1642 when Boston threatens to sue him for the land granted him in 1640 (Boston Records, Second Rep. of Rec. Com. pp. 58, 59, 71, 82, 84). Probably the house was built in 1641.

The Brackett homestead is a very old structure, at least in the northwest end of it. Its situation near the shore and its structural character mark it as a very ancient building. The Wheelwright grant may have included the land upon which it is built. Captain Richard Brackett was granted permission to sell house and garden in Boston, June 1, 1638 (Bost. Rec. 34). If he then bought land in Braintree it was just when Wheelwright was disposing of his grant, and Captain Brackett may have been part purchaser. But this is all conjecture; I have not been able to find any facts. I am not at all confident, even, that the earliest Capt. Richard Brackett owned and occupied this old homestead. His land seems to be in this neighborhood (Br. Rec. p. 5), and all the way up Town Brook to the county road (Hancock Street) the land at a later time is in the possession of his descendants. Elm Street was early called the road "leading to Capt. Richard Brackett's Landing." But which Capt. Richard is it, — there was another Richard born in 1707, — and where is the landing?

The Adams mansion, built originally about 1730, "as the summer resort of a West India planter," says Mr. C. F. Adams the younger, was sequestered as Tory property after the Revolution, and bought by John Adams in 1785. Leonard Vassall was the name of this planter, a rigid Episcopalian, who in his will before his marriage, in 1737, made provision that his widow should have the use and improvement of his real estate during her continuing "a professed member of the Episcopal Church of England." The house he built "still contains one room panelled from floor to ceiling in solid St. Domingo mahogany. Originally it was a small dwelling, constructed on a plan not unusual in the tropics, with a kitchen and all domestic arrangements behind the house and in a separate building. In itself it contained only parlors and sleeping-rooms; but gradually it was added to, until the original house is now lost in the wide front and deep gabled

Lewis Vassall 1737—Vassall 1743—Cranch—G...

House of the Rev. John Wilson
From a sketch by Miss E. S. Quincy, taken in 1846

This house stood on Hancock St. Braintree now Quincy and was built about 1640 on the tract of land granted him by the Colony

Situated on the Taylor Farm, near the corner of Beale and Hancock Streets, Wollaston wings of the later structure. In this house John Adams died; and in the same room in it were celebrated his own golden wedding, and the golden wedding of his son and grandson."

It was a temptation not easily resisted to include among the pictures a view of a corner of this drawing-room. Such was its appearance while the house was occupied by the late Mr. and Mrs. C. F. Adams. The last event of which it was the scene was the burial service over the remains of Mrs. Adams. Vocal is that room with great memories. What gatherings of notable persons have been there! What high converse has been held there! On the walls are the portraits of the two Presidents and their consorts, and others famous in history.

Lewis Vassall, a brother of Leonard, built a house on the other side of the town similar to the one bought by John Adams. He died in 1743, having occupied the house about ten years. In 1749 the estate was sold at auction to "James Virchild of the Island of St. Christophers, Esq." Some years afterward Richard Cranch sold his farm back of President's Hill, and took up his residence in the Virchild house. He lived here till his death in 1811. John Greenleaf, who married Lucy, a daughter of Richard Cranch, subsequently bought the estate. For many years it was the homestead of the Cranches and the Greenleafs. The estate is now owned by Mr. James Edwards. The old house was removed in the year 1857 to Water Street, and a fine modern structure built in its place. A painting of the house in its original situation was made while still occupied by the Greenleafs, by Mr. C. P. Cranch, and from that the heliotype is taken.

The old houses distinguished as the birthplaces of Presidents John and John Quincy Adams are described as excellent specimens of the dwellings of the farmers of the earliest period of our history. Two houses so notable there are not besides in the whole country. Not only are they famous as the birthplaces of two of our greater Chief Magistrates, but as the scene of that beautifully heroic and devout domestic life portrayed in the letters of Abigail Adams.

A history of considerable length might be written about the Quincy mansion, but here one must limit himself to mere dates. The diary of John Marshall tells us that "June 14, 1706, we raised Mr.

Quinzey's house," — but whether this was the beginning of the mansion or the building of an addition to it is a little uncertain. Before this, on March 22, 1685–86, Samuel Sewall, according to an entry in his diary, "Lodged in the lower room of Unkle Quinsey's new house." Was this "new house" the oldest part of the present mansion, or was it the little farm-house with the gambrel roof standing a little to the south of the mansion? I am inclined to the opinion that the "new house" of 1685–86 is the old part of the mansion, and that the farm-house was there from the beginning. Indeed, with respect to that farm-house the thought recurs again and again that it is the original Coddington house. He had a house near here; the brook was first called "Coddington's Brook;" and the land he sold was in part on the south of the brook, extending as far as the "buring ground." The Quinceys seem to be in Boston till after the departure of Coddington. But all this is aside from the real interest which attaches to the Quincy mansion as the birthplace and home of so many eminent persons.

The farm-house of the Rev. John Wilson is included among the pictures because it is a good specimen of the old architecture, and because it was built by the minister whose parish had its centre in Boston and its confines in this distant region. He was the first to receive a grant of land within the limits of our old township. He was given a great farm here, and built him the house in the picture. The house he never occupied, but descendants of his lived in it and it was long in the family. With regard to the sketch reproduced for this book, I quote the following from a letter received from Mr. Thomas Minns of Boston in response to inquiries made of him: —

"I had given considerable attention to the genealogy of the Rev. John Wilson, and knew that the later generations of the Quincys were descended from him, and that the thousand acres of land granted him by the Colony adjoined the Quincy estate.

"When Mr. A. B. Ellis was writing his history of the First Church in Boston, I suggested that he should write to the Quincys and ask if they had anything about the Rev. John Wilson.

"This drew out interesting letters from the late Hon. Josiah Quincy and his sister Miss E. S. Quincy, and one of her letters was accompanied by a sketch of the house and barn made by her in 1846.

"Mr. E. Whitefield, an artist, was known to me as having produced several interesting volumes of 'Homes of our Forefathers,' and I suggested to Mr. Ellis that he should make this sketch for his book, and it will be found at page 101. Mr. Whitefield went to Quincy, saw Miss Quincy, who kindly accompanied him to the spot; and he then and there made this sketch, adding the house and barn from the picture made by Miss Quincy in 1846. I think the cellar of the house still remains."

To one who is familiar with the history of the Quincy family, it must seem an omission that portraits of other eminent bearers of the name are not inserted in this volume. There is Edmund Quincy, third of the name, born in 1627, conspicuously active in the affairs of town and church, the first major and lieutenant-colonel in Braintree, and one of the Committee of Safety which in 1688 formed the provisional government of the colony until the arrival of the new charter from William and Mary. He bequeathed to our church a silver cup as a token of his love for it; his entire life was spent in this place. A portrait of him is something to be wished for; none, however, is in existence, as far as I can learn. Of his son, another Edmund, born in 1681, there is a portrait extant; but it is said not to be worthy the man. He is the Edmund the Rev. Mr. Hancock writes of so affectionately. A notable man he was in his day, made colonel of the Suffolk regiment, — Braintree was then part of Suffolk County, — and commissioned judge of the Superior Court of Judicature. At the age of fifty-eight he was appointed by the State special agent to represent its interests at the court of Great Britain with respect to the boundary line of Massachusetts and New Hampshire; he died in London while executing his trust. He was in his day the most prominent man in First Church. It is "Colonel Edmund Quinsey, Esqr.," who is chosen moderator of the first meeting of "ye north-end Precinct," and he continues to be the favorite presiding officer and leading spirit of it till after the building of the Hancock meeting-house, which he did so much to further. He is interesting to us, also, as the father of "Dorothy Q.;" and to afford a glimpse of them and their times I cannot do better than to insert here a letter written to the damsel when she was visiting at Springfield. Mr. Quincy was living in the mansion by the brook, and Dorothy was fifteen years of age, a little older than when her portrait was painted, as Dr. Holmes guesses. The letter is taken from Miss Eliza Susan Quincy's Memoir of Edmund Quincy, published in the New England Historical and Genealogical Register for April, 1884.

BRAINTREE, July 8, 1724.

MY DEAR DAUGHTER, — This is to bring you the good news of my safe return home, Commencement day, in the evening, and finding your mother in good health.

With this you will have from your sister Betsey the things you wrote for by me, and from your brother Edmund a small present. My child, you are peculiarly favored among your friends in these parts in having a good word spoken of you, and good wishes made for you by everybody; let this hint be improved only to quicken and encourage you in virtue and a good life.

My love to all the family in which you are, with your Mother's and Grandmothers' also, to them and you.

I am your dear and loving father,

E. QUINCY.

Half a yard of muslin being too little for two head-dresses, your sister has sent you one yard wanting half a quarter, which cost ten and sixpence, — and the thread (lace) cost fourteen shillings; so much I paid for, and 't is the best thread and muslin of the price.

Some time before the departure of Edmund Quincy for England, Major John Quincy was frequently appointed moderator of the North Precinct (or church) meetings; he also, for years, was a favorite presiding officer. There is a portrait of him as a child in the possession of the Adams family; but it is the "major" we want to see, — the "colonel," the "speaker of the House," the patriot who "was as much esteemed and respected as any man in the province." As such, unfortunately, his face is not to be looked upon. It was in honor of him that the North Precinct was named Quincy. Mr. C. F. Adams the younger writes of this incident as follows: —

"When in 1792 the original town of Braintree was subdivided, the Rev. Anthony Wibird was requested to give a name to the place; but he refusing, a similar request was made to the Hon. Richard Cranch, who recommended its being called Quincy, in honor of Col. John Quincy. Nor was this the only form in which the name was perpetuated. Colonel Quincy had two children, a son named Norton in honor of his mother's family, and a daughter who became in time the wife of William Smith, of Weymouth. Among the children of this couple was one who in October, 1764, married John Adams. In July, 1767, as old John Quincy lay dying at Mount Wollaston, this granddaughter of his gave birth to a son, and when, the next day, as was then the practice, the child was baptized, its grandmother, who was present at its birth, requested that it might be called after her father. Long afterwards, the child thus named wrote of this incident: 'It was filial tenderness that gave the name. It was the name of one passing from earth to immortality. These have been among the strongest links of my attachment to the name of Quincy, and have been to me through life a perpetual admonition to do nothing unworthy of it.'"

The portrait of the William Smith, above spoken of, is placed in the group of some particularly connected with First Church for two reasons: First, because that minister is closely related to many persons prominent in our history, — one daughter, as we have seen, marrying John Adams, and another marrying Richard Cranch. The second reason is an antiquarian one, the desire to save the likeness from possible destruction.

MOSES FISKE'S AUTOGRAPH.

Mr. WILLIAM BLAKE TRASK transcribed lately the sermon which the Rev. Moses Fiske preached June 4, 1694, before the Ancient and Honorable Artillery Company. This was done by vote of the company, and it is now for the first time printed. While engaged in this work, Mr. Trask searched out the material for a quite exhaustive life of minister Fiske, with a view to publication. What he has written is still in MSS. He found an autograph of Mr. Fiske in Worcester, which he at once had engraved. This he has kindly permitted me to use.

Moses Fiske

www.ingramcontent.com/pod-product-compliance
Lightning Source LLC
Chambersburg PA
CBHW020905230426
43666CB00008B/1315